J. C. Ryle's concern in the 19th century that many Christians were concerned with 'politics, or controversy, or party spirit, or worldliness' instead of godliness is just as relevant today—if not more so. His *Holiness: Its Nature, Hindrances, Difficulties, and Roots* is perhaps the first resource I would give someone on the importance and nature of progressive sanctification. It is clear, theologically insightful, and deeply edifying. Ryle shows that truly encountering the free grace of God will compel us to fight for growth in personal holiness. This abridged version will make Ryle's classic work even more accessible to a wider audience.

Gavin Ortlund
Research fellow, Trinity Evangelical Divinity School
Author of *Ascending Toward the Beatific Vision: Heaven as the Climax of Anselm's Proslogion*

I was in my late teens when I came across J. C. Ryle as an author. I collected and devoured his various titles, including his classic volume, *Holiness.* It was compelling reading and it gives me great joy to commend this rewritten and abridged version of Ryle's writing on the subject for a new generation of readers. It will inform your mind, warm your heart and strengthen your will, knowing that God's promised Holy Spirit continues to empower the saints for service to their King. Would that all bishops of the Church of England could so clearly articulate such a pattern for discipleship in such a captivating manner!

Glenn N Davies
Archbishop of Sydney, Anglican Diocese of Sydney

Bishops Ryle's exhortations on the lifelong pursuit of holiness are some of the best ever written. He overflows with a burning love for Christ and a desire to grow more and more in Christlikeness, while facing up to the stark realities of the seriousness of sin. Thoroughly biblical and practically applied, none can read Ryle without being shaken from their spiritual slumber.

Andrew Atherstone
Latimer Research Fellow, Wycliffe Hall, Oxford

GRACE
ESSENTIALS

ASPECTS OF
HOLINESS
HOLINESS

Unless otherwise indicated Scripture quotations are taken from the New International Version, Coryright © 1973, 1978, 1984 by International Bible Society. Used by permission of Hodder and Stoughton, a member of the Hodder Headlines Group. All rights reserved.

paperback ISBN 978-1-5271-0104-3
epub ISBN 978-1-5271-0163-0
mobi ISBN 978-1-5271-0164-7

First Published in 1999 as *Aspects of Holiness*
This revised edition published in 2018
in the
Christian Heritage Imprint
by
Christian Focus Publications Ltd,
Geanies House, Fearn, Ross-shire,
IV20 1TW, Scotland, U.K.
www.christianfocus.com
and
Grace Publications Trust
7 Arlington Way
London, EC1R 1XA, England.
www.gracepublications.co.uk

Cover design by Pete Barnsley
Printed by Bell & Bain, Glasgow.

GRACE
ESSENTIALS

ASPECTS OF
HOLINESS
HOLINESS

J. C. RYLE

CHRISTIAN
HERITAGE

Contents

Introduction by Bishop Ryle

For a number of years I have had the conviction that practical holiness and complete self-consecration to God are being neglected. Godliness has been smothered by worldliness, personal devotion to Christ hardly exists and standards of Christian living have been lowered. The importance of making *the teaching about God our Saviour attractive* (Titus 2:10) has been forgotten.

Professing good evangelical doctrine is useless unless it is accompanied by a holy life. The insincerity of claiming to be a Bible-believing Christian without holy living is soon recognised as a sham which brings contempt for our religion.

It is of utmost importance, however, that the whole subject should be understood in the light of Bible teaching. My intention in this book is to try and explain what the Scripture actually teaches on the subject. And since there are several wrong ideas on the subject being taught by some, I begin by alerting you to those errors.

1. Is it wise to teach, as some do, that the holiness of believers comes by faith only, and not at all by the believer's personal effort?

No well-taught Christian will ever deny that faith in Christ is the beginning of all holiness. Until we believe in Him we have no holiness at all. But surely the Scripture teaches us that the believer needs personal exertion in this matter, as well as faith. The same apostle who wrote, *The life I live in the body, I live by faith in the Son of God* (Gal. 2:20) also wrote, *I beat my body and make it my slave* (1 Cor. 9:27). In other places we read, *Let us purify ourselves ... Let us make every effort... Let us run with perseverance* (2 Cor. 7:1; Heb. 4:11; 12:1).

There is a difference between how faith justifies[1] us and how it sanctifies[2] us, according to Scripture teaching. Justifying faith is a grace which simply trusts, rests, leans on Christ (Rom. 4:5). All who simply believe are justified. Sanctifying faith is a grace which, like the mainspring of a clock, moves the believer toward holiness; *the only thing that counts is faith expressing itself through love* (Gal. 5:6). Nowhere does the New Testament speak of 'holiness by faith'. Whereas we are told that we are justified by faith without the deeds of the law, nowhere are we told that we are sanctified without the deeds of the law. On the contrary, we learn that, *faith by itself, if it is not accompanied by action, is dead* (James 2:17).

2. Is it wise to make so little, as some do, of the many practical exhortations to holiness found in the Sermon on the Mount and in the latter part of Paul's epistles?

1   **Justify/Justification**. To justify a person is to declare that person to be righteous. It is a forensic word, that is, connected with lawcourts; a judge justifies a person, declaring that person to be in the right. God justifies believers on the basis of what Jesus Christ has done for His people. (From *A Dictionary of Theological terms*, published by Grace Publications Trust)

2   **Sanctify/Sanctification**. Sanctification is that basic work of God's Holy Spirit in believers by which He makes believers increasingly holy (set apart for God). The work is never completed in this life, but will be complete in heaven. (From *A Dictionary of Theological terms*, published by Grace Publications Trust)

No well-taught believer will dispute the need of a daily walk with God, of a regular habit of coming to the Lord Jesus Christ in prayer and meditation. But the New Testament is not content to teach us in such general terms. Instead, we find it speaks of many details and particular things.

The use of our tongues, of our tempers, our natural inclinations, our conduct as parents or children, masters or servants, husbands, wives, rulers, subjects, our demeanour in sickness or in health, in riches or in poverty — all these are matters about which the Bible speaks in detail. Holiness is much more than tears and sighs, bodily excitement, a quickened pulse, passionate attachment to some preacher or religious group. It is being *conformed to the likeness of [God's] Son* (Rom. 8:29); it is something capable of being seen by others, in the detail of our character, habits and daily behaviour.

3. Is it wise to teach that it is possible for a believer to reach a standard of complete holiness in this life?

There is no doubt that believers are constantly urged, in Scripture, to *aim for perfection* (2 Cor. 13:11). But I have yet to find a single passage in the Bible which teaches that a complete and entire freedom from sin is possible, or has ever been reached, in this life by any believer. A comparative perfection is possible; but as to a literal and absolute perfection, none of the greatest saints of God in any age have ever claimed it. And the great saints of Bible history — David, Paul, John — had no hesitation in declaring that they were conscious of weakness and sin in their own hearts.

I must think that those who claim sinless perfection in this life know very little of the nature of sin, or of the holiness of God. I protest against such unbiblical teaching, for it is a dangerous delusion. It disgusts discerning people and alienates them from religion for they see the notion is false. It depresses some of the best of God's children, who feel far from reaching such perfection and it makes weak believers feel proud, when they fancy they are something when they are not.

4. Is it wise to assert so positively, as some do, that the seventh chapter of Romans describes, not the experience of a saint, but the experience of an unregenerate person?

This is a point which has been in dispute ever since the time of Paul. But it must be said that all the Reformers, the Puritans, and many other students of Scripture all agree that Paul here describes the experience of a Christian believer. (Ryle indicates a list of names, including Haldane and Owen, who defend the position that Paul is writing of his own present experience). To disregard the weight of the opinions of such an array of Reformers and Puritans is surely unwise?

5. Is it wise to understand the expression 'Christ in us' in such a way that it gives the expression an unbiblical importance?

Undoubtedly the expression is scriptural; (Rom. 8:10; Gal. 2:20; Eph. 3:17; Col. 3:11). And some have actually suggested that we are to understand this truth as meaning that the believer is not responsible for what he or she does, because it is Christ in them who does everything! That cannot be right. To make this claim is to ignore the fact that the presence of Christ in the believer is by the presence of the Holy Spirit in them. Christ, as our risen High Priest, is specially at God's right hand interceding for His people until He comes again. It is the Holy Spirit who is the *Counsellor to be with you for ever* (John 14:16) to carry out His special work of urging us on in sanctification. Never forget that a distorted truth, as some have distorted this truth of 'Christ in us', is the starting point of dangerous heresies.

6. Is it wise to separate between conversion and consecration, or 'the higher life', as some have done?

There is a view that there are two kinds of Christians, the converted and those enjoying the higher life of complete consecration. It is suggested that there can be sudden instantaneous leaps from conversion to consecration, as though the believer needs a second conversion. I suspect that those who use such language have a low view of conversion. The only division spoken of by the Word of God is that between believer and unbeliever, between the spiritually alive and the spiritually dead. Within each of these two groups there are undoubtedly varying measures of sin and grace. And for the believer there needs to be gradual growth in grace, in knowledge, and in spiritual mindedness. But sudden instantaneous leaps from conversion to consecration I do not see in the Bible.

I doubt, indeed, whether a person can be converted if he or she is not consecrated to God. More consecrated he or she can always be, as God's grace grows in them. But to suggest one can experience new birth and not be consecrated suggests to me a poor understanding of what conversion means.

7. Is it wise to teach believers that they ought not to think of struggling against sin, but rather should yield themselves to God?

The expression *yield yourselves* occurs in only one place in the New Testament (Rom. 6:13-19, King James Authorised version). In those verses *yielding ourselves* is spoken of as a duty of believers. But the word 'yield' does not have the sense of putting ourselves passively into the hands of another person. It has much more the sense of actively presenting ourselves for the use of another, as *Offer yourselves to God* (Rom. 6:13, New International version).

In any case, twenty or thirty other passages of Scripture teach that believers are not to sit still, but rise up and work. A warfare, a fight, a soldier's life, a wrestling, are spoken of as the characteristic of the Christian life. Why else should we need to put on *the armour of God?* (Eph. 6:10-18). People will persist in confounding two things that differ. In Justification we are told to believe, *only* believe; in Sanctification we are told to watch, pray and fight.

I leave my introduction here with much anxiety. There is an attitude among professing Christians today (i.e. the nineteenth century — Ed.) which fills me with concern for the future. There is an amazing ignorance of Scripture among many, with a consequent lack of true religion. There is an increased taste for the sensational; thousands will crowd to hear a new voice and a new doctrine, without considering whether what they hear is true. Crowds and crying and an incessant rousing of the emotions are the only things many care for. So long as the preacher is 'clever' and 'earnest', hundreds seem to think it must be alright.

It is my heart's desire and my daily prayer that personal holiness will greatly increase among professing Christians. And I trust that all who endeavour to promote it will adhere closely to what the Scripture teaches and carefully distinguish between doctrines that differ. What the Lord says is, *if you utter worthy, not worthless, words you will be my spokesman* (Jer. 15:19).

Chapter 1. Sin

... sin is lawlessness (1 John 3:4)

A right knowledge of sin is the basis of a true understanding of Christianity. Without that such truths as justification, conversion[1] and sanctification are only words and names. The first thing that God does when He draws people to Himself is to give them an inner awareness that they are guilty sinners. As the creation of the world began with the coming of light (Gen. 1:3) so this new awareness of sin is the beginning of the spiritual recreation of a person. God shines into our hearts by the Holy Spirit and then our spiritual life begins (2 Cor. 4:6).

1. Some definitions of sin

Sin is that vast moral disease which affects the whole human race. A sin consists in doing, saying, thinking or imagining anything which does not conform perfectly with the mind and law of God. The slightest outward or inward departure from complete agreement with God's revealed will and character is a sin and at once makes us guilty in God's sight. It is all too easy to break God's law in thought or desire when there is no

---

1. **Conversion**. The Hebrew and Greek words translated 'to convert' have the meaning of 'to turn' 'to change' i.e. to turn from sin to God. Conversion is the act of turning after regeneration. (From *A Dictionary of Theological terms*, published by Grace Publications Trust.)

visible act of wickedness. Our Lord settled that point beyond dispute in his Sermon on the Mount (Matt. 5:21-28).

It is also easy to break God's law by omitting to do what He requires. Again, Jesus made this very clear: *I was hungry and you gave me nothing to eat, thirsty and you gave me nothing to drink* (Matt. 25:41-43). And I must remind you that it is possible to commit sin and yet be ignorant of it. God's people Israel were taught that there are sins of ignorance (Lev. 4) which our Lord confirmed when He said, *the one who does not know and does things deserving punishment will be beaten...* (Luke 12:48). We do well to remember that our imperfect knowledge is not the true measure of our sinfulness!

2. The origin and source of sin

Our sinfulness does not begin from outside us, but from within. It is not the result of bad training in early years; it is not picked up from bad companions and bad examples. No! It is a family disease with which we are born, inherited from our first parents Adam and Eve. *Sin entered the world through one man ...* (Rom. 5:12). The most beautiful baby born this year is not 'a little innocent thing', but a little sinner. Only watch it develop and you will soon see in it the germs of deceit, bad temper, selfishness, self-will, obstinacy, greed, jealousy, passion — which if indulged and left alone will grow as rapidly as weeds in the garden. Who taught the child these things? The Bible alone can answer this question! *From within, out of men's hearts, come evil thoughts, sexual immorality, theft, murder, adultery, greed, malice, deceit, lewdness, envy, slander, arrogance and folly. All these evils come from inside and make a man 'unclean'* (Mark 7:21-23).

3. Concerning the extent of sin

We must make no mistake about this; the only safe ground for our understanding is what the Bible teaches. *Every inclination of the thoughts of [every person's] heart was only evil all the time* (Gen. 6:5); *The heart is deceitful above all things* (Jer. 17:9). Sin is a disease which runs through every faculty of our minds; the understanding, the affections, the reasoning powers, the will, are all infected. Even the conscience is blinded so that it cannot be depended upon as a sure guide to right behaviour, unless it is enlightened by the Holy Spirit.

All this may be hidden by an outward show of courtesy. It is true that many human beings have noble faculties and show immense capacity for excellence in art, science and literature. But the fact remains that in spiritual things we are 'dead'. We naturally have no fear or love of God in our hearts. What is best in us is so mixed with corruption that the contrast only serves to show the extent of sin in us.

The power of sin is such that, even after we have experienced conversion by the working of the Holy Spirit in our lives, we still feel its strength. We never rid ourselves of the roots of sin in us. Where believers are concerned, all we can be certain of is that sin is weakened and kept in check by God's grace[2] in us. But the battle we must fight daily between the desires of the flesh and of the spirit testifies to the enormous power and vitality of sin.

I know no stronger proof of the biblical account of mankind's origin than this universality of sin. If we accept that all human beings have descended from one pair, and that

---

2. **Grace.** God's favour to His people in saving them through Christ. The term 'free grace' emphasises that salvation comes because of God's grace alone and from nothing in believers. (From *A Dictionary of Theological terms*, published by Grace Publications Trust.)

pair rebelled against God, then the state of our human nature is easily accounted for. If we deny the Genesis story, as some do, then we have difficulty in explaining the amazing extent and power of sin today.

Happy is the believer who understands the fact of sin, and can say 'Thanks be to God who gives us the victory through Jesus Christ our Lord' while never forgetting to watch and pray lest he or she falls into temptation.

4. Concerning the wickedness of sin

I do not think that we, with our inadequate conception of sin, can ever grasp the exceeding hideousness of it in God's pure sight. A blind person cannot tell the difference between a famous work of art and a crude village sign; a deaf man cannot tell the difference between a simple whistle and a great organ.

Let us settle it in our minds that God's eyes are *too pure to look on evil; [he] cannot tolerate wrong* (Hab. 1:13) and that therefore *the soul who sins is the one who will die* (Ezek. 18:4). Even from the lips of Jesus we have the words, *They will go away to eternal punishment* (Matt. 25:46). These are terrible words when we consider they are written in the book of a merciful God!

But supremely, no proof of the foulness of sin is so overwhelming and unanswerable as the cross and the cry of our Lord, *My God, my God, why have you forsaken me?* (Matt. 27:46). Not until Christ comes the second time shall we fully realise the 'sinfulness of sin'.

5. Concerning the deceitfulness of sin

The deceitfulness of sin can be shown by our readiness to make excuses for it and to minimise its guilt. We say, 'It is only a little sin ... God is merciful ... we meant well ... one cannot be so particular ... where is the harm?' What do we mean? We mean that we are trying to cheat ourselves into believing that sin is not really so sinful. I fear we do not realise the extreme subtlety of sin. It rarely presents itself as sin, at first.

What real reasons we have for humiliation and self-abasement; reasons to consider the need of a change of heart — the change which the Bible calls regeneration[3], new birth and conversion. On the other hand, how thankful we ought to be for the gospel message which tells us of the remedy for our disease. We need not be afraid to study the nature, origin, power, extent and vileness of sin if, at the same time, we look at the salvation provided for us in Jesus Christ. *Where sin increased, grace increased all the more* (Rom. 5:20).

6. Some practical uses to which the doctrine of sin may be put

a) In the first place a scriptural view of sin is one of the best antidotes to a vague and hazy kind of theology which is so common: 'something about Christ, something about grace, something about faith'. Such a vague theology neither exercises any influence on daily life nor gives peace in death. Those who submit to such a theology often realise too late that there is nothing solid or real about their religion.

---

3.   **Regeneration.** The action by which God gives spiritual life to a person; being 'born again', becoming a 'new creation'. (From *A Dictionary of Theological terms*, published by Grace Publications Trust.)

People will never set their faces decidedly toward heaven and live like pilgrims until they really feel they are in danger of hell because of their sin. We may depend upon it, people will never come to Jesus, stay with and live for Him, unless they know why they need to come. Those whom the Holy Spirit draws to Christ are those whom He has convicted of their sinfulness.

b) A scriptural view of sin is the best antidote to liberal and modernist theology. The tendency of this theology is to reject all dogmatic statements of truth and to try and convince us that everything is true, everybody is right and eventually everybody will be saved. The atonement[4] of Christ, the personality of the devil, the miracles of which Scripture speaks, the reality and eternity of future punishment — all these truths have been pushed aside in the mistaken belief that to do so will make Christianity more acceptable to modern ideas.

c) A scriptural view of sin is the best antidote to a ceremonial, formal kind of Christianity. A little child is satisfied with toys and dolls so long as it is not hungry. So it is with us in matters of the soul. Once a person understands their sin and their need of a Saviour, then music, flowers, candles, incense, banners and man-made ceremonies will seem to him or her a sad waste of time.

d) A scriptural view of sin is the best antidote to theories of sinless perfection. By all means let us aim high. But if people

---

4. **Atonement.** Atonement is an inclusive word to describe all that Christ did towards God and towards His people by His death. Christ kept the law of God during His earthly life and by His death satisfied the demands made on sinners by the law of God. (From *A Dictionary of Theological terms*, published by Grace Publications Trust.)

really mean to tell us that here in this world a believer can live for years in unbroken communion with God, I must say that such a view is unscriptural and dangerous. *If we claim to be without sin, we deceive ourselves and the truth is not in us* (1 John 1:8).

e) A scriptural view of sin is the best antidote to low views of personal holiness. It has long been my sorrowful conviction that the standard of daily life among professing Christians has been gradually falling. It may be that the increase of wealth has introduced a plague of worldliness and the love of ease. It may be that religious controversy has dried up our spiritual life. Whatever the reason, there has recently (i.e. the nineteenth century — Ed.) been a lower standard of personal holiness than there used to be in the days of our fathers. I am convinced that the first step towards attaining a higher standard of holiness is to realise more fully the amazing sinfulness of sin.

Chapter 2. Sanctification[1]

Sanctify them by the truth; your word is truth (John 17:17)

It is God's will that you should be sanctified (1 Thess. 4:3)

This is a subject of the utmost importance. Unless we are sanctified, according to the Bible we shall not be saved. There are three things necessary to our salvation — justification, regeneration and sanctification. For a person to lack any one of these three means that in God's sight they are not true believers. None dying in that condition will be found in heaven. So a careful examination of the subject as a great doctrine of the gospel is necessary for our soul's welfare.

1. The true nature of sanctification

Sanctification is the working of the Holy Spirit in anyone called to be a believer. The Spirit works to create an awareness of sinfulness and then an awareness of God's goodness in wiping away guilt by the work of Jesus Christ. The Spirit

---

1. **Sanctification**, in Scripture, has a twofold significance. The first is a separation and dedication of things for the use of God only, as in the Old Testament priesthood and the utensils used in tabernacle and temple. The second is a sanctification or holiness which is the result of a person being dedicated to God. It is the obedient actions of such a person toward God. It is this latter which is the subject of this chapter. (From *A Dictionary of Theological terms*, published by Grace Publications Trust.)

works through the Scripture to separate believers from a natural love of sin and worldliness and to make them Christ-like in daily life.

Jesus not only lived and died and rose again to provide justification and forgiveness for the sins of His people, but also undertook to provide everything that His people's spiritual life requires. He sends the Holy Spirit to their hearts to replace the desire for sin by a desire for holiness. Christ has said, *For them I sanctify myself, that they too may be truly sanctified* (John 17:19) and Paul writes, *Christ loved the church and gave himself up for her to make her holy, cleansing her by the washing of water through the word* (Eph. 5:25,26). Believers, reading these verses with understanding, will realise that Christ both justifies and sanctifies us also. And I want to put to you now a number of statements which will define the exact nature of sanctification.

a) Sanctification is the invariable result of the vital union with Christ which faith gives to every true believer. Christ has said, *If a man remains in me and I in him, he will bear much fruit* (John 15:5). Whoever bears no spiritual fruit in daily life is not in Christ. Any supposed union with Christ which produces no effect in the daily life is worthless. *Whoever claims to live in him* [i.e. in Christ] *must walk as Jesus did* (1 John 2:6).

b) Sanctification is the inseparable consequence of regeneration. Whoever is born again and made a new creature lives a new life. Where there is no holy life there has been no rebirth; where there is no sanctification there is no regeneration. *Everyone who does what is right has been born of him* (1 John 2:29). *No-one who is born of God will continue to sin ... he cannot go on sinning, because he has been born of God* (1 John 3:9).

c) Sanctification is the only certain evidence of the indwelling Spirit which is essential for the salvation of a true believer. *If anyone does not have the Spirit of Christ, he does not belong to Christ* (Rom. 8:9). The Spirit is never idle but always makes His presence known by the 'fruit' He causes to develop in the character and life (Gal. 5:22,23). If this fruit is missing then the presence of spiritual life must be in doubt. Just as we know there is wind by the effects it produces, so we may know the Spirit is in a person by the effects He produces in their life. *Those who are led by the Spirit of God* [and only they] *are sons of God* (Rom. 8:14).

d) Sanctification is the only sure mark of those who are the elect of God. The names and number of God's elect people are secrets known only to Him. But one thing is clear from the Scripture; elect men and women may be distinguished by holy lives. *For he* [God] *chose us in him* [Christ] *before the creation of the world to be holy and blameless in his sight* (Eph. 1:4). Of course, many who make a fair show of religion may turn out at last to be hypocrites. But where there is not at least some appearance of sanctification we may be certain there is no election.

e) Sanctification is a thing that will always be seen. A tree is known by its fruit. A truly sanctified believer will be clothed with humility even though he or she may be conscious of defects in their spiritual lives. A so-called 'saint' in whose life nothing can be seen but worldliness is a kind of monster not recognised in the Bible.

f) Sanctification is a thing for which every believer is responsible. Believers, as children of God, have the knowledge of the gospel message and a new life and hope within themselves. *His divine power has given us everything we need for life and godliness through our knowledge of him who called us* (2 Pet. 1:3). If Christians nevertheless are not holy, whose fault is it but their own? If they are not sanctified, on whom can they throw the blame but themselves? If the Saviour of sinners gives us renewing grace may we not be sure that He expects us to use His gifts? Not to do so is to be among those who, sadly, grieve the Spirit.

g) Sanctification is a thing which is capable of growth and development. A Christian cannot be more pardoned, more justified than when first believing but he or she may certainly be more sanctified. God's holiest saints all agree: they see more, and know more, and feel more, and do more, and repent more, and believe more, as they go on in the spiritual life and walk more and more closely with God. We are to *grow in the grace and knowledge of our Lord and Saviour Jesus Christ* (2 Pet. 3:18).

h) Sanctification is a thing which depends upon the diligent use of scriptural means, sometimes called 'the means of grace'. I have in view, when I speak of 'means', Bible reading, private and public prayer times, public worship, hearing the Bible explained, and regular reception of the Lord's Supper. I can find no record of any eminent saint who ever neglected these things. I should as soon expect a farmer to prosper who contented himself with sowing his fields and never looking at them again till harvest, as expect a believer to attain holiness who was not regularly paying attention to these means.

i) Sanctification is a thing which does not prevent much spiritual struggle. By spiritual struggle I mean that *the sinful nature desires what is contrary to the Spirit, and the Spirit what is contrary to the sinful nature. They are in conflict with each other* (Gal. 5:17). A sense of spiritual struggle and mental discomfort are no proof that a person is not sanctified; rather the reverse — they prove that a person is spiritually alive. A believer may have a peaceful conscience, while there is a war raging within! I believe what I say is confirmed by the language of Paul in Romans chapter seven. I am quite satisfied that he does not describe there the experience of an unconverted person, or of a young Christian, but of an old established saint in close communion with God. (This was also the view of the Reformers, the Puritans including Haldane and Owen, and a number of Bible scholars since — Ed.)

We can look forward to the absence of this struggle in heaven, but never will enjoy freedom from it in this life. Even after regeneration our souls are still infected by the remains of sin.

j) Sanctification can never justify a person, yet it pleases God. The holiest actions of the saintliest person still suffer from defects and imperfections; they are only 'splendid sins' as one has said. The motive may be wrong, the performance defective. The only righteousness by which we can present ourselves to God is a perfect righteousness, and such is found in our Lord alone. His perfection and not ours, His work and not ours, are our justification and our only right to heaven!

At the same time, we are assured that the right actions of believers are pleasing to God even though imperfect. As a parent is pleased with the imperfect efforts of a little child to please, so is our Father pleased even with the imperfect efforts of His children. He looks at the intention of our actions, not merely their quantity and quality.

k) Sanctification is a thing which will be absolutely necessary in the great day of judgement. When God calls us to the final judgement, evidence that our faith in Christ is genuine will be the only thing that will save us from condemnation. The question will not be how we talked and what we professed, but how we lived and what we did. *For we must all appear before the judgment seat of Christ, that each one may receive what is due to him for the things done while in the body, whether good or bad* (2 Cor. 5:10).

l) Sanctification is necessary to prepare us for heaven. Most people hope to go to heaven when they die, but few take the trouble to consider if they would enjoy being there! Heaven is essentially a holy place — its inhabitants are holy, its occupations are holy. To be happy in heaven it is obvious that we should have prepared for being there while here on earth. When an eagle is happy in an iron cage, when a sheep is happy in the water, when an owl is happy in the blaze of the noonday sun, when a fish is happy on dry land, then, and not till then, can I admit that an unsanctified person could be happy in heaven.

2. What are the visible marks of a sanctified person?

a) Sanctification is more than talking about religion. Some people are so familiar with the words and phrases of the gospel, and talk so fluently about them, that they convince others they are believers. God does not want His people to be mere empty tubs, echoing gongs or clashing cymbals. *Let us not love with words or tongue but with actions and in truth* (1 John 3:18).

b) Sanctification is not just enjoying temporary religious feelings. Special services and revival meetings can attract a lot of attention and we ought to thank God when they present the gospel message to so many people. But these things have attendant dangers as well as advantages. Wherever wheat is sown the devil will sow tares. We need to beware of religious excitement causing people to feel a temporary attraction to the Lord. After a little while they can fall back, and then are harder and worse than before. Let us urge everyone who shows a new interest in Christianity to be content with nothing short of a deep sanctifying work of the Holy Spirit.

c) Sanctification is not just the occasional performance of right actions. Many sincere people take pleasure in doing what they feel are religious acts from time to time. But I am afraid that in many cases this external religiosity is no substitute for inward holiness. I feel that there is need of very plain speaking on this subject. There may be an immense amount of 'bodily service' while there is not the least real sanctification.

d) Sanctification does not consist in retiring from daily life in the world. In every age there have been those who believe that to retire into seclusion from the world is a highway to sanctification. But wherever we go we carry with us that source of evil — our hearts. True holiness is not a frail plant which can only survive in a plant nursery, but is a strong, hardy thing which can flourish in normal daily life. True holiness does not make a Christian evade difficulties, but face and overcome them.

e) Sanctification shows itself in a continual respect for what God requires of us. Whoever pretends to be a saint, while sneering at the Ten Commandments and thinks nothing of breaking any of them, is seriously deluded and will find it hard to prove he or she is a saint in the last day!

f) Sanctification will show itself in a constant effort to do Christ's will. His practical requirements are found throughout the Gospels, and in the Sermon on the Mount. Our Lord continually taught what His disciples ought to be and do. *You are my friends if you do what I command* (John 15:14) were His words. We still serve this same Lord.

g) Sanctification will show itself in a desire to live up to the standard which Paul set before the churches. That standard is to be found in the closing chapters of nearly all his letters. I defy anyone to read Paul's writings carefully without finding in them a large number of plain, practical directions about the Christian's duty in every relation of life. These directions were written down by the inspiration[2] of God for the guidance of professing Christians.

h) Sanctification will show itself in attentiveness to all the spiritual graces which our Lord so beautifully displayed. *As I have loved you, so you must love one another. By this all men will know that you are my disciples* (John 13:34-35). Peter, writing to believers, makes the same point: ... *if you suffer for doing good ... to this you were called, because Christ suffered for you, leaving you an example, that you should follow in his steps*

---

2. **Inspiration of Scripture** means that the original Scriptures were 'breathed out' by God (2 Tim.3:16) so that the words that were written were the words God wanted written. (From *A Dictionary of Theological terms*, published by Grace Publications Trust.)

(1 Pet. 2:20,21). Paul names nine graces in his list of the fruit of the Spirit in Galatians 5:22-23. It is nonsense to pretend to sanctification unless we show these things in our lives. Not all believers exhibit equally all these marks, but they are the biblical standard to which every believer should aim.

3. Lastly, I wish to consider the difference between justification and sanctification, showing how they agree and how they differ

(i) How do they agree?

a) Both originate as free gifts from God to believers.

b) They are the result of the work of Christ, from which justifying pardon and sanctifying holiness both flow.

c) Both are to be found in the same believer; the justified are always sanctified, the sanctified are always justified.

d) Both begin at the same time. The moment a person is justified, he or she also begins to be sanctified.

e) Both are alike necessary to salvation. No one reaches heaven without holiness as well as pardon.

(ii) How do they differ?

a) Justification is reckoning a person to be righteous[3] for the sake of Jesus Christ. It is something done **for** the believer.

---

3. **Righteous/righteousness.** The Hebrew word translated 'righteous' originally meant 'straight'. The corresponding Greek word referred to anything which conformed to the law. Christ is the only person who has perfectly kept God's law, and because He is also God His righteousness is infinite and can be credited to those who believe in Him. (From *A Dictionary of Theological terms*, published by Grace Publications Trust.)

Sanctification is actually making a person inwardly righteous by the Holy Spirit; it is something done **in** the believer.

b) The righteousness believers have in justification is not their own but Christ's. The righteousness of sanctification is the believer's own.

c) In justification, religious works that we do have no significance. Simple faith in Christ is all. In sanctification, we act; we fight, watch, pray, strive, and labour!

d) Justification is something that is complete and finished. Sanctification is never completed until we reach heaven.

e) Justification does not grow or increase. Believers are as much justified in the hour of first belief as they will ever be. Sanctification is a movement in our souls; it grows and increases throughout this life.

f) Justification has to do with our standing in God's sight; sanctification has to do with our state of soul.

g) Justification gives us authority to enter heaven; sanctification prepares us to enjoy the life of heaven.

h) Justification is God's work outside us; it is invisible to other people. Sanctification is God's work within us; it will be obvious to people around us.

I commend these distinctions to my readers. Never let the two words be confused or the distinctions between them be forgotten. They are two separate things; yet whoever has the one must have both.

4. What practical thoughts ought this matter of sanctification bring to our minds?

Without holiness no-one will see the Lord (Heb. 12:14).

a) For one thing, let us awake to the peril of not being holy! Without sanctification there is no salvation. What an enormous amount of so-called religion is perfectly useless, lacking true holiness! What are our tastes, our choices, our desires? This is the great testing question.

b) If we want to be sanctified we must go to Christ as sinners, and tell Him of our desperate need.

c) We must continue as we began — we must come to Christ again and again. He is the head from which every member of His body must be supplied. Believers who seem at a standstill in sanctification are generally neglecting regular communion with Christ.

d) We must not expect too much from our hearts in this life. Sinners we were when we began this road, sinners we shall find we still are as we continue: renewed, pardoned, justified certainly — yet sinners to the very last.

e) Let us, nevertheless, make much of striving for the highest standard of holiness. Holiness is happiness, and those who get through life most comfortably are believers who are sanctified. *Great peace have they who love your law, and nothing can make them stumble* (Ps. 119:165).

Chapter 3. Holiness

Without holiness no-one will see the Lord (Heb. 12:14)

Are we holy? Shall we see the Lord? Solomon tells us that there is *a time to weep and a time to laugh ... a time to be silent and a time to speak* (Eccles. 3:4,7). But the time to be holy is now! No matter who or what we are, we must be holy now. In this hurrying, bustling world, I ask to be heard about this matter.

1. What practical holiness is — and what sort of people are those whom God calls holy

a) Holiness is the habit of agreeing with the will of God. It is loving what He loves and hating what He hates. It is measuring everything in this life by the standards of God's Word, the Bible. Whoever agrees most entirely with God is the most holy person.

b) Holiness is when a person endeavours to keep from every known evil and seeks to keep every known requirement of God. It is to have a mind which loves God's ways. Holiness is to feel like the psalmist when he said, *because I consider all your precepts right, I hate every wrong path* (Ps. 119:128). And Paul could say, *in my inner being I delight in God's law* (Rom. 7:22).

c) Holiness is striving to be like Jesus, living a life of faith in Jesus, drawing from Him daily peace and strength. Holiness is to have *the mind of Christ* (1 Cor. 2:16) and so being *conformed to the likeness of his* [God's] *Son* (Rom. 8:29). Christ was forgiving, unselfish, loving, humble, and obedient to God. Christ was a faithful witness for the truth, denying Himself to serve others, meek and patient under insults, bold in denouncing sin, going about doing good, frequently in prayer. These are the Christ-like virtues to follow for our daily living. *Whoever claims to live in him* [in God] *must walk as Jesus did* (1 John 2:6). Much time would be saved, and much sin prevented, if people would oftener ask, What would Christ have said or done in this situation?

d) Holy people are meek, gentle, patient, slow to talk of 'standing on their rights'. We see good examples of this in Moses when Aaron and Miriam spoke against him, Numbers 12:3, and in David when Shimei cursed him, 2 Sam. 16:10.

e) Holy people are not self-indulgent. They will not allow wrong desires, affections, or immoral inclinations to control their lives. As Jesus Himself warned His followers, *Be careful, or your hearts will be weighed down with dissipation, drunkenness and the anxieties of life* (Luke 21:34). (And nowadays this warning would undoubtedly apply to sexual promiscuity, alcohol, drugs or anything else which is addictive — Ed.).

f) Holy people are full of love — the kind of love that Jesus spoke about in the Sermon on the Mount and which Paul described in 1 Corinthians 13. Where there is this love, lying, cheating, stealing, hurting other people in any way, is impossible!

g) Holiness is love in action. This is not merely a matter of doing no harm; it is to do good. Dorcas was *always doing good and helping the poor* (Acts 9:36). Paul was able to write to the believers at Corinth, *I will very gladly spend for you everything I have and expend myself as well* (2 Cor. 12:15).

h) Holiness seeks purity of mind and heart. Such a person will dread all uncleanness of spirit, and avoid anything which might lead him or her into impurity. Who can be careless about these things, when David (2 Sam. 11) — the man after God's own heart — committed such serious sin? Under the old ceremonial laws of Israel whoever merely touched a bone, or dead body, was at once unclean in God's sight. Few Christians are ever too careful about purity of mind and heart!

i) Holiness is to have a deep respect for God and His ways. Like a child who wishes to behave in ways that please the parents, so the believer loves God and wants to please Him. Nehemiah gives us a fine example of this when he declined to act in a certain way saying, *Out of reverence for God I did not act like that* (Neh. 5:15).

j) Holy people are humble people, always esteeming others better than themselves. Such people will always see more evil in their own hearts than in the lives of others. They know what Abraham meant when he said, *I am nothing but dust and ashes* (Gen. 18:27), and Jacob, when he said, *I am unworthy of all the kindness and faithfulness you have shown your servant* (Gen. 32:10), or Paul, when he said, *Christ Jesus came into the world to save sinners — of whom I am the worst* (1 Tim. 1:15).

k) Holy people are faithful and reliable in their duties and relationships. *Whatever you do, work at it with all your heart, as working for the Lord, not for men* (Col. 3:23) wrote Paul to the church in Colosse. Holy people should aim at doing everything well — good husbands, good wives, good parents, good children, good in private, good in public, good at work and good in the home. Holiness is worth little if it is not worth this much.

l) Finally, holy people are spiritually-minded people. They recognise that this life is a preparation for life in heaven. This means they are able to accept that the only things of true value in this world are those which fit us for the next.

We have looked at the character of those who are rightly called 'holy'. But let no believer be discouraged by such a list of aims. Holiness is only attained with much effort. Growth in holiness brings an increased consciousness of sin. Sanctification is always a progressive work; at best, it is an imperfect work. The holiest saints may have many a blemish in God's sight. Light will never shine without some clouds and even the sun itself has spots on its face!

But while accepting the weak and sinful side of human nature, the picture of holiness given here can still be the goal of every believer. It is what they strive to be, if it is not what they are.

2. Reasons why practical holiness is important

a) We must be holy because God commands it, in the Bible. The Lord Jesus said to His disciples, *I tell you that unless your righteousness surpasses that of the Pharisees and the teachers*

of the law, you will certainly not enter the kingdom of heaven
(Matt. 5:20). And again, *Be perfect, therefore, as your heavenly
Father is perfect* (Matt. 5:48). Peter wrote, also to believers, *As
he who called you is holy, so be holy in all you do; for it is written:
"Be holy, because I am holy"* (1 Pet. 1:15-16).

b) We must be holy because it was to make us holy that Christ
came into the world. *Christ loved the church*, wrote Paul,
*and gave himself up for her to make her holy, having cleansed
her* (Eph. 5:25,26). Christ died not merely to save us from
the guilt of our sins but also to save us from its power. Are
believers said to be 'elect'? It is through the sanctifying work
of the Spirit. Are they 'predestined'? It is *to be conformed to the
likeness of his* [God's] *Son* (Rom. 8:29). Are they chosen? It is
that they may *be holy and blameless in his sight* (Eph. 1:4). Are
they called? It is *to a holy life* (2 Tim. 1:9). Are they afflicted?
It is the case that God *disciplines us for our good, that we may
share in his holiness* (Heb. 12:10). Jesus is the complete Saviour
who does not merely take away the guilt of a believer's sin,
but also breaks its power over the believer enabling him or
her to be holy.

c) Holiness is the evidence that faith in Christ is real. James
warns that there is such a thing as a dead faith; true faith will
bear fruit; it will make us holy (James 2:17,18). I suspect that
people die in the same condition as they have lived. Those
only who live a holy life are the ones who die in righteousness.

d) Holiness of life proves that our love to the Lord is sincere.
The words of Jesus make this very clear: *If you love me you will
obey what I command* (John 14:15). *He who loves me will be
loved by my Father, and I too will love him and show myself to*

him (John 14:21). *As the Father has loved me, so have I loved you. Now remain in my love* (John 15:9). Plainer words than these would be difficult to find!

e) Holiness is the evidence that we are God's children. Jesus said to the Jews who claimed to be God's children: *If God were your Father, you would love me* (John 8:42). We must prove by our actions that we do indeed belong to God's family.

f) By being holy we help others to search for holiness. Our lives will always be an example for good or evil, a silent sermon that others can read. It is sad if our sermon is for the devil's cause and not for God's. O, for the sake of others, if for no other reason, let us strive to be holy! *If any ... do not believe the word, they may be won over without words ... when they see the purity and reverence of your lives* (1 Pet. 3:1,2).

g) Our present comfort depends upon our holiness. Too often we forget the connection between sin and sorrow. We forget that God's plan is that our happiness depends upon how we fulfil His will. *Let us not love with words or tongue but with actions and in truth. This then is how we ... set our hearts at rest in his* [God's] *presence* (1 John 3:18,19). When the disciples deserted Christ and fled they escaped danger but they were miserable. When, later, they confessed Him boldly before men they rejoiced *because they had been counted worthy of suffering disgrace for the Name* (Acts 5:41).

h) Without holiness on earth we shall never be prepared for holiness in heaven. Our characters are not altered by death. We will rise on the judgement day having exactly the same character as that with which we died. Only those who are prepared for heaven will be happy in heaven. Suppose for a moment you were allowed to enter heaven without holiness — what would you do there? Holiness is everywhere in heaven; what enjoyment could you find there?

Let me remind you of the verse at the beginning of this chapter: *Without holiness no-one will see the Lord.* Surely such words prompt us to self-examination. Are we holy? Do we think, feel and act as we know Christ would think, feel and act? *Everyone who has this hope in him purifies himself, just as he* [Christ] *is pure* (1 John 3:3). To purify ourselves is a difficult thing to do, but it is essential.

I do not ask, 'Do you attend church regularly? Have you been baptized? Do you call yourself a Christian?' I do not ask whether you approve the holy lives of others. I do not even ask if you can talk about holy things — I ask something more: 'Are you yourself holy this very day?'

3. Some advice to those who desire to be holy

a) Begin with Christ. Sometimes people try to make themselves holy, and a sad work they make of it. All we need to do is to turn to Christ; to come to Him by faith and be joined to Him. *Apart from me you can do nothing* (John 15:5) is how Jesus Himself expressed it.

b) Holiness is Christ's special gift to His people. It is the result of being united to Him. If it is holiness you desire then I urge you, wait for nothing; wait for nobody; go to Christ.

c) To continue in holiness, we must abide in Christ. He is the physician to whom you must go daily if you would keep spiritually well. He is the manna which you must daily eat, the rock from whom you must continually drink. As Paul wrote, *I can do everything through him who gives me strength* (Phil. 4:13).

May all who read these pages know these things by experience and not merely by hearsay!

Chapter 4. The Fight

Fight the good fight of the faith (1 Tim. 6:12)

Whoever wishes to understand the nature of holiness must understand that the Christian is engaged in a fight. It is this spiritual warfare which Paul meant when he wrote to Timothy, *Fight the good fight of the faith.*

1. True Christianity is a fight

I speak of 'true' Christianity. There are many who would call themselves Christians who know nothing of spiritual struggle, conflict or self-denial. They may be married in church, buried in church, call themselves 'Christians', but you never see any 'fight' about their religion. Theirs is not the religion which the Lord Jesus founded and which the apostles preached. It is not a religion which produces holiness.

With whom does the Christian fight? Not with other Christians! As a general rule, the cause of sin is only helped when Christians waste their strength in quarrelling with one another. The true Christian fights a constant battle against *the world, the flesh and the devil.* These are the chief enemies of true Christians, for, with corrupt hearts, a busy devil and a world always seeking to entrap them, Christians must either fight or be lost.

a) Christians must fight 'the flesh'. Even after conversion all believers still carry within them a nature prone to evil and emotional feelings which can lead them astray. To deal with such temptations there is the need for daily spiritual struggle and daily earnest prayer. As Paul wrote to the believers in Colosse: *Put to death, therefore, whatever belongs to your earthly nature: sexual immorality, impurity, lust, evil desires and greed, which is idolatry* (Col. 3:5). (And one could add things which in our day are likely to be addictive, such as various kinds of gambling, drugs, etc. — Ed.)

b) Christians must fight 'the world'. The subtle influence of the world's ungodly love of material things is hard to resist. Christians may fear the unbelieving world's laughter or blame; may wish to copy the behaviour of unbelieving people, may fear to appear extreme in the eyes of the world — but these are the spiritual enemies they must fight. *You adulterous people, don't you know that friendship with the world is hatred towards God? Anyone who chooses to be a friend of the world becomes an enemy of God* (James 4:4). Christians must fight the world!

c) Christians must fight the devil. We must not doubt the reality of the devil. He is alive; he never sleeps; he is the Christian's unseen enemy. *Satan has asked to sift you as wheat* (Luke 22:31). This enemy must be resisted every day if we wish to be saved. *Be self-controlled and alert. Your enemy the devil prowls around like a roaring lion looking for someone to devour. Resist him, standing firm in the faith...* (1 Pet. 5:8-9).

This fight is absolutely necessary: There is no such thing as neutrality in this matter. We have no choice. To be at peace with the world, the flesh and the devil is to be opposed to God. We must either fight — or be lost!

This fight is for every Christian — whatever nationality, class, age or rank. All are living in a world full of traps and pit-falls. All have a busy devil near them. All have the influence of their old natures before their conversion. All must fight!

The fight is ceaseless; it is until we die. The Christian's enemies take no holidays, never weary and never sleep. Conflict is the constant companion of those who wish to be holy. It is a sad thing when a so-called Christian knows nothing about this spiritual battle.

At the same time, Christians may take comfort from the knowledge that experiencing this inward fight is a good sign, for it can be evidence that they are on the right path to reach holiness of life. So I repeat; let us take comfort from this struggle. There are two great marks which identify the true Christian; an inner spiritual warfare, and an inner sense of peace! Here we are concerned with the former of these.

2. True Christianity is a fight of faith

In this respect, Christian warfare is utterly unlike the conflicts of this world. It does not depend upon physical strength and does not use military weapons. Success in this spiritual warfare depends upon spiritual faith.

a) Success depends entirely on belief in the Word of God — the Bible. Christian soldiers do what they do, think as they think, hope what they hope, for one simple reason — they believe what is taught in the Bible. Faith is the very backbone of their existence. There is no such thing as right living without right believing.

b) There needs to be a special faith in the Lord Jesus Christ and what He has done. If believers look only at their own weaknesses, and at the strength of the world against them, they might well despair. But instead they have a mighty Saviour, by whose sacrificial death they are redeemed, and by whose continual intercession they are preserved, from whom to draw their strength.

According to the degree of this faith a Christian fights well, or poorly. Whoever has most faith will be the happiest Christian soldier. The more faith, the more victory! I think it impossible to overrate the value and importance of this faith. Read chapter eleven of the letter to the Hebrews, in the Bible, and see how early Christians held fast to their faith in every situation. Believing in an unseen Jesus was their strength. *Lord, increase our faith!* (Luke 17:5).

3. True Christianity is a good fight

It may seem strange to use the word 'good' of any warfare. But the Christian fight is good because there is no evil in it. I must not hide from anyone the fact that if they would be holy they must fight. But I also want my readers to know that the Bible calls the Christian fight 'good' for real reasons.

a) It is a good fight because it is fought under the best of generals! The leader and commander of all true Christians is the Lord Jesus Christ. And He has perfect wisdom, infinite love and almighty power. He never errs in judgement, never makes any useless moves. Those whom He has redeemed are far too precious to Him to be wasted or thrown away. Surely this is good?

b) The Christian's fight is good because it is fought with the best of helps. The Holy Spirit lives in each believer. No believer goes to this spiritual warfare in his or her own strength. God the Father guards every believer. God the Son prays for every believer. God the Spirit guides and teaches every believer. That is a threefold help which can never fail. Surely this is good?

c) It is a good fight because it is fought with the best of promises. *Sin shall not be your master ... The God of peace will soon crush Satan under your feet ... He who began a good work in you will carry it on to completion until the day of Christ Jesus* (Rom. 6:14; 16:20; Phil. 1:6). Surely those are good promises?

d) It is a good fight because it will have the best of results. No soldiers of Christ are ever missing, or left dead on the battlefield. Every believer is, without exception, *more than conqueror through him who loved us* (Rom. 8:37). No Christian soldier will be missing from heaven. Surely this is good?

e) The Christian's fight is good because it does good to those that fight it. Earthly wars bring out the worst side of human nature. They harden consciences and destroy morality. But spiritual warfare brings out the best things in the believer. It brings humility, lessens selfishness and worldliness and draws believers to think much of spiritual things. Surely this is good?

f) This fight does good to the world. An army fighting its way across some country does terrible damage to that country and its people. But Christian soldiers are a blessing to others wherever they live. They raise the level of morality, and check dishonesty. Even unbelievers are obliged to respect them. The presence of even a few Christians is a blessing wherever they are. Surely this is good?

g) This fight is good because it ends in a glorious reward for all who fight it. Who can estimate the good things that our Commander has in store for all His faithful soldiers? Whatever He gives will last for ever, for it is beyond the reach of death. The believer will receive a *crown of glory that will never fade away* (1 Pet. 5:4). Surely this is good?

So I urge you, if you are not already a Christian soldier, become one now! Fight the good fight of faith so that you may be happy as well as safe. Why be a slave to this world and its ways? There is room for you in Christ's army — choose liberty and fight to the last. May we never forget that without fighting there can be no holiness while we live and no crown of glory when we die!

Chapter 5. The Cost

Suppose one of you wants to build a tower. Will he not first sit down and estimate the cost to see if he has enough money to complete it? (Luke 14:28)

It is a good sign if we want to be holy — we may thank God for putting that desire in our hearts. At the same time, we ought to think seriously about how being a Christian will really affect our lives. Christ's way to eternal life is a way of great comfort, but it is also a narrow way in which the cross comes before the crown!

1. I will show what it costs to be a true Christian

I am not discussing what it costs to save a Christian's soul. I know that it cost nothing less than the life-blood of the Son of God to provide an atonement for sin and so redeem a person from hell. I want to consider what believers are ready to give up for a life of service to Christ.

I grant that it costs little to be a merely nominal Christian. To attend a place of worship on a Sunday and to be tolerably moral during the week is a cheap and easy Christianity; there is no self-denial or self-sacrifice in it. But it does cost something to be a real Christian — there are enemies to be overcome, battles to be fought, sacrifices to be made, temptations to be resisted. That is why it is important for us to count the cost.

a) There is a cost to our self-righteousness. We must put away all pride and all conceit about what we think is our own goodness. We are saved only by the goodness and merit of another — Jesus Christ. Without Him our morality, our praying, our Bible study, attendance at meetings for worship, all add up to nothing. We have to know that in ourselves we are poor, helpless sinners. So, to be a true Christian will cost us our self-righteousness.

b) There is a cost to our sins. We must give up every action which is wrong in God's sight. Whether small or great, whether publicly known or secret, all sins must be renounced. *Take your evil deeds out of my sight! Stop doing wrong, learn to do right!* (Isa. 1:16). This will be hard to do. Our sins are often as dear to us as our children; we love them, hug them, cling to them, delight in them! Christ is willing to receive sinners but He will not receive them if they stick to their sins. To be a true Christian will cost us our sins.

c) There is a cost to our love of ease. If we wish to be successful as believers on our journey to heaven, constant effort will be necessary. We must be careful in our behaviour every moment of the day — careful about each thought, each word, each deed. We will need to be careful about our prayers, our Bible study, our use of the 'means of grace'[1]. This also sounds hard

1. **The Means of Grace.** Those activities of the Christian believer by means of which faith is strengthened, spiritual knowledge increased, and devotion to Christ encouraged: e.g. Bible reading, prayer, Christian worship with other believers, the Lord's Supper, and witness to others concerning the faith. (From *A Dictionary of Theological terms*, published by Grace Publications Trust)

advice. We dislike anything which requires struggle. But we can have no gains without pains. To be a true Christian will cost us our easy living.

d) It may cost us popularity with our neighbours. If our main aim is to please God, then we may have to accept much ill-will from other people. People may dismiss us as fools, or fanatics. Jesus said, *Remember the words I spoke to you: No servant is greater than his master. If they persecute me, they will persecute you also* (John 15:20). This will be hard to bear. It is always unpleasant to be spoken against. But it must be endured. To be a true Christian may cost us the goodwill of our non-Christian neighbours.

Let us remember that a religion which costs nothing is worth nothing. A cheap Christianity without a cross would, in the end, be a useless Christianity without a crown!

2. I will show you why it is important to count the cost

There is one group of people for whom estimating the cost of being a true Christian is of great importance. They are not ignorant of religion. They know much about it, but their faith is not strong. They may have picked up their knowledge 'secondhand' and not by personal experience. They may have been reared in a religious family. But such persons are in real danger, for their religion requires little effort from them. When they near the end of life, and try to make some last efforts to turn to God, they will find that repentance is not such an easy thing as they had imagined. These people need to look at examples in the Bible of those who did not count the full cost of what God required, and in the end they died in their sins.

a) Thousands of the children of Israel perished in the wilderness between Egypt and Canaan, because they had not counted the cost. They left Egypt eagerly and full of zeal. They had thought that the Promised Land would be theirs at once. But when they experienced difficulties their enthusiasm left them and their courage failed. They had not counted the cost. They lost their faith and died in their sins.

b) For want of counting the cost many of those who listened to our Lord after a while *turned back and no longer followed him* (John 6:66). They had seen His miracles and thought that the Kingdom of God would appear immediately. But when they found there were hard doctrines to be believed and hard work to be done, their faith collapsed. They had not counted the cost.

c) For want of counting the cost King Herod returned to his old sins and destroyed his soul. He had heard John the Baptist preach and liked what he heard. He was interested — and even honoured John as a holy man. But his faith could not control his lust, nor accept the criticisms of his guests (Mark 6:19-28). He had not counted the cost of living according to John's holy teaching.

d) For want of counting the cost, Demas deserted Paul because he was unwilling to give up his friendship of this world for the friendship of God. *Demas, because he loved this world, has deserted me,* wrote Paul (2 Tim. 4:10). Evidently Demas had not counted the cost, when he joined Paul's team of workers.

e) For want of counting the cost many people who hear powerful preaching will for a while appear to be changed. They are stirred to claim a spiritual experience they have not really known. And when the novelty is gone they drift away from the congregation of believers (Matt. 13:20-21). They did not count the cost.

f) For want of counting the cost many who seem to be converted at large revivals[2] and special 'evangelistic missions' fail to maintain their faith. They fail to understand that religion is more than a sensation of 'coming to Christ'. When they find, after a time, that there is a cross to be carried, that our hearts are deceitful and that Satan is always near us, they return to Christless ways of living. They have never really counted the cost (Matt. 13:20-21).

g) For want of counting the cost the children of Christian parents often fail to develop as Christians themselves. From

2. **Revivals**. Ryle has a long note at this point on the subject of revivals, which has been omitted from this abridgement. He seems to be referring to the type of special evangelistic meetings sometimes mistakenly called 'Revival meetings'. Ryle has no criticism of those periods of revival when the power of the Holy Spirit is experienced in remarkable ways by individuals in whole areas of a country. But he is critical of the suggestion that simply by holding 'Revival meetings' conversions can be assured, and of the simplistic type of ministry often heard in such meetings.

He stresses that while he longs to see sinners converted, and urges believers to witness to that end, nevertheless it is the full teaching of the Christian faith which needs to be explained, rather than simple exhortations for people to 'come to Christ'. He insists that repentance needs to be stressed, that 'instantaneous' conversions are not to be regarded as common, that counting the cost should be emphasised, and that one needs to take care not to mistake merely human emotional feelings affecting large groups of people, for a lasting work of the Holy Spirit in individual hearts.

their earliest years they have known Bible truths, but without really experiencing them for themselves. And once away from home they begin to discover worldly pleasures and have no further time for Christian things. They have not counted the cost — perhaps they had never been taught that there was a cost!

I would be so bold as to say that it would be good if the duty of counting the cost was more frequently taught than it is. People ought to be told honestly what it is they are taking up, if they express a desire to serve Christ. Let us not be like a dishonest recruiting sergeant for the army who speaks only about the uniform, the pay and the glory, and says nothing about the enemies, the battle, and the wounds.

3. How can we count the cost rightly?

There is nothing to make us afraid if we count the cost of being a Christian in a right way. Any cost required of us can be paid, if our faith is strong. We have only to read of such biblical characters as Noah, Moses and Paul to realise that without a strong faith in God the cost of what He asked of them would have been too great for them to pay. It may cost much to be a true Christian, but against that we must always put the reward of heaven's glory.

a) So let us compare the profit and the loss. We may lose some things of this temporary world, but gain the eternal salvation of our souls.

b) Compare the praise and the blame. Other people may want to blame you, but, as His child, you have the praise of God!

c) Compare the friends and the enemies. On one side is the devil, and wicked people. But on the other is the favour and the friendship of the Lord Jesus Christ, who has defeated the devil.

d) Compare the life that is now, with the life that is to come. There may be struggles and trials now, but they last only for a few years. On the other hand, there is the everlasting life of heaven, where there is no sin, no struggle or trial.

e) Compare the pleasures of sin and the blessing of God's service. The pleasures of this world are unsatisfying; they shine for a few moments and then are gone. They depend so much upon happy circumstances. But the blessings of God are for ever, and do not depend upon earthly circumstances.

f) Count up and compare the troubles a Christian may have and those that are in store for the ungodly. Nothing that the Christian may be called to suffer compares with the eternal wrath of God upon the wicked.

Such sums as these are often not done correctly, or even not done at all. Many cannot make up their minds whether it is worth serving Christ. The great secret of counting the cost in a right way is to have a strong faith. I urge you, my reader, to consider whether your present religion costs you anything at all. I urge you to consider what it has cost God to bring salvation to sinners in this world. I urge you to consider how, when in the glory of heaven, you may look back and marvel that you could ever think the cost was too much for you to have suffered!

Chapter 6. Growth

Grow in the grace and knowledge of our Lord and Saviour Jesus Christ (2 Pet 3:18)

This is a vital matter for those who are serious about their commitment to holiness. They need to sometimes ask, Am I making progress in my religion? Do I grow? Perhaps birthdays, or at Christmas, or before joining in the Lord's Supper are suitable times for such self-examination. There are three points about this spiritual growth which I wish to stress.

1. The reality of growth in spirituality

There is such a thing as growth in grace. In saying this, I would like to make it clear that I do not mean that we, by our own efforts, can make any difference to our justification in God's sight. We cannot ever be more pardoned, more forgiven, more justified than we are at the first moment we believe. The growth which I refer to is growth in the graces given to us by the Holy Spirit — our repentance, our faith, hope, love, humility, zeal and courage. We can, and should, make continual spiritual progress by growth in each of these graces.

Growth in grace is taught in the Bible. *Your faith is growing more and more, and the love every one of you has for each other is increasing* (2 Thess. 1:3). *Bearing fruit in every good work, growing in the knowledge of God* (Col. 1:10). I pray *that your*

59

love may abound more and more (Phil. 1:9). And there are many more such exhortations.

But personal experience also confirms that the possibility of growth in grace is a fact. The difference between the degree of faith and knowledge when first converted, and what is true after some years of walking with the Lord, is evidence in itself that there has been growth. I want to emphasise that our own best interests are in this matter of growth. For example:

a) Growing in grace is the best evidence of spiritual health. Anything that is alive proves its health by steady progress in growth. What does not grow is not alive.

b) Growing in grace is one way to be happy in our religion. There is a link between our comfort and our holiness. The believer who feels the most joy and peace in believing and has the clearest 'witness of the Spirit' in his heart (Rom. 8:16) is the believer who is growing spiritually.

c) Growing in grace is one secret of our usefulness to others. Our influence on others depends greatly upon what they see in us. The believer who sets the world thinking is the believer who is continually improving and going forward.

d) Growing in grace pleases God. It may seem remarkable that anything we do can please God. But Jesus told His disciples, *This is to my Father's glory, that you bear much fruit, showing yourselves to be my disciples* (John 15:8). The Lord takes pleasure in all His people, but especially in those that grow spiritually.

e) But, above all else, let us realise that growing in grace is not only possible, but is something for which we are accountable. Whose fault is it if a believer does not grow? It is clearly not the fault of God. Believers have a duty to grow. Neglect of growth robs the believer of privileges, grieves the Spirit, and dulls the soul. We ourselves are to blame, and no one else, if we are not growing spiritually.

2. The results of growth in spirituality

How may we find out whether we are growing in grace, or not? I answer that there are certain results of such growth, and wherever we see such consequences we see a growing soul. Let me indicate some of these results.

a) One result of growing in grace is the possession of a greater humility. As we draw nearer to God, and know more of His holiness and perfection, so the more we are aware of our own unworthiness in His sight. We feel the centurion's words (Matt. 8:8) could be ours — *Lord, I do not deserve to have you come under my roof.* Or, in the words of the Prodigal Son (Luke 15:19) *I am no longer worthy to be called your son.* The more believers mature and ripen for heaven's glory so the more, like corn, they hang down their heads.

b) Another result of growing in grace is increased love toward the Lord Jesus Christ which, in turn, deepens faith in Him. No doubt the believer thinks much of Christ when first believing. But growth in grace makes Christ more and more desirable. This is a result of growth to look for!

c) Another result of growing in grace is an increase of holiness in the life. There is more watchfulness over weakness in our character. There is a stronger resistance to the devil and to sin. It is a sign of not growing in grace if we find ourselves less troubled about sin.

d) Another result of growing in grace is more spirituality in our desires and thoughts. The believer who is growing will faithfully discharge responsibilities of home and life. But the best loved things will be spiritual things. Amusements and ideas which once were all-important will seem to lose their value. Such things may not be sinful in themselves, but will gradually seem trifling things to the growing believer.

e) Another result of growing in grace is a greater love toward all people, but especially toward other believers. A growing soul will try to put the best interpretation on another person's conduct. The surest sign of a decrease in grace is a willingness to find faults and see weak points in other people.

f) The last result of growing in grace which I will mention is growing interest in evangelism. How we think about and work for missions, at home and abroad, is a most reliable sign of the growth of our souls. If we want to know whether or not we are growing spiritually, let us see if there is a growing concern for the salvation of others.

3. The resources to be used to assist spiritual growth

Whoever wishes to grow in grace must use the God-given means of growth. *Every good and perfect gift is from above* (James 1:17). This is as true of the resources for the encouragement of growth, as it is of every other gift of God. Since God has made these resources available it is the responsibility of every Christian believer to make best use of them.

a) Our private prayers, our Bible reading and our private meditations are the best helps towards the growth of the soul. To be careless and lazy about these things is to be wrong everywhere! I know we live in an age full of dangers — much hurry and pressure of many activities. I suspect that English Christians two hundred years ago read their Bibles more than they do today (Ryle wrote at the end of the 19th century — Ed.). Personal and private religion must receive our first attention if we wish our souls to grow.

b) Also essential to spiritual growth is the careful use of the public means of grace. Regular meetings for praise and worship of God, joining in the Lord's Supper, hearing the message of the Scriptures preached — these are public resources to assist growth in grace. The danger is that our familiarity with these things is apt to make us careless. If we would grow we must be on our guard lest the regular doing of the same things causes us to lose our appetite for them.

c) Watchfulness over our conduct in the small things of life is important. Life is made up of small things: our everyday moods, the fulfilment of our regular duties, the way we use our time, are all important matters. We must aim to have a Christianity which, like the sap of a tree, runs through every twig and leaf of our character and sanctifies all.

d) There must be caution about the people with whom we mix and the friendships we form. Disease can be passed from one person to another, but health can not. If, among our friends, there are those who are not friends of God how will our spiritual growth be helped? Mistakes in friendships and marriage engagements are the whole reason why some believers have not grown. *Bad company corrupts good character* (1 Cor. 15:33).

e) There is one more thing which I believe is of great importance. Regular communion with the Lord is essential to spiritual growth. I do not mean merely the attendance at the public means of grace. I mean a growing understanding of the relationships between the Lord and ourselves as believers. He is the Bridegroom to us as His bride; He is the Head to us as His members; He is the Physician to us as His patients; He is the Advocate for us as His clients; He is the Shepherd for us as His sheep; He is the Master for us as His disciples. Getting close to the Lord in these relationships is what I mean as something essential to spiritual growth. We must learn what it means to say, with Paul, *For to me, to live is Christ* (Phil. 1:21). We must realise what it is to turn to Him first in every need, to talk to Him about every difficulty, to consult Him about every step, and to spread before Him all our sorrows and joys.

Last of all, if we are growing in grace, or earnestly seeking to grow, we must be prepared for hardship. We may have to go through many trials and much affliction in this life. One of our Lord's striking sayings, of the relationship between Himself and His disciples, is, *Every branch that does bear fruit he prunes [trims clean] so that it will be even more fruitful* (John 15:2). When God corrects us by some circumstance it is meant for our instruction and our growth! *No discipline seems pleasant at the time, but painful. Later on however, it produces a harvest of righteousness and peace for those who have been trained by it* (Heb. 12:11). So let us ask ourselves the question: In our religion, in the things which concern our peace of mind, in our holiness — are we alive? Are we therefore growing?

Chapter 7. A Certain Hope

I am already being poured out like a drink offering, and the time has come for my departure. I have fought the good fight, I have finished the race, I have kept the faith. Now there is in store for me the crown of righteousness, which the Lord, the righteous Judge, will award to me on that day — and not only to me, but also to all who have longed for his appearing (2 Tim 4:6-8)

In these verses the apostle Paul speaks without any hesitation or doubt, about the past, the present and the future. He has no shame about his past as a Christian; he has no fear of his near departure from this life; and he has no doubt about the outcome of the future judgement after death.

Since God had turned him towards heaven he had aimed to serve his Lord consistently. His conscience was clear — and although no one can enter heaven by the merits of a good conscience alone, it does give comfort when passing from this world to the next. And he could look forward to the day of judgement with courageous certainty. There is no hesitancy about his words — no 'I hope' or 'perhaps'. Paul had assurance[1] about his salvation.

---

1. **Assurance.** Believers may know with certainty that they are believers, children of God, born again, possessors of eternal life. Believers base their assurance on several things:
   - The promises of God; e.g. (John 6:37)
   - The inward witness of the Holy Spirit (Rom. 8:16)

There are four things that I want to say about this matter of the believer possessing a certain hope, this assurance of salvation. And I do so humbly, realising that this is a difficult subject.

1. This assurance is a true and scriptural thing

Assurance is a gift of the Holy Spirit, which every believer in Christ ought to seek. It seems to me the Bible teaches that true believers may reach such a state of faith in Christ that they will be entirely confident about the eventual safety of their souls. There are, however, some churches[2] which insist that it is not possible for a believer to be so confident, and that, if they are, they are deceived.

It is true that some may presume that their salvation is sure, who have no real reason to say so. Yet there is verse after verse in the Bible which insist that assurance is a true gift of the Holy Spirit. So my reply to those who deny the existence of assurance is simply this — what does the Bible say?

*I **know** that my Redeemer lives, and that in the end he will stand upon the earth. And after my skin has been destroyed, yet in my flesh **I will** see God* (Job 19:25-26).

*Even though I walk through the valley of the shadow of death, **I will fear no evil**, for you are with me* (Ps. 23:4).

- The moral evidences of salvation (Matt. 7:20)
- Three tests in John's first epistle: Right belief — 3:23; 4:2; 5:5,10; Right behaviour — 1:5,6; 2:3; 3:6,9; Love — 4:7,8 (From *A Dictionary of Theological Terms,* published by Grace Publications Trust).

2. This would be true of the teaching of the Roman Catholic Church and of some small Protestant groups also, who fear that assurance is not possible without presumption.

There are many more references to people experiencing such a certain hope — see Isaiah 26:3; 32:17; Romans 8:28-39; 2 Corinthians 5:1,6; Colossians 2:2; 2 Timothy 1:12; Hebrews 6:11;10:22; 2 Peter 1:10; 1 John 3:14; 5:13. In all these passages we find humility and assurance side by side. And the assurance of which they speak is always a confidence in God, never in themselves. To those who dislike the idea of a believer being assured I say, It cannot be presumption to follow in the footsteps of Job, the Psalmist, Isaiah, Paul, Peter and John. They were humble minded men and yet they spoke of having a certainty of hope. How can it be wrong to be certain when God has given us His sure promises?

2. A believer may have saving faith and yet not know assurance

I believe it is of great importance to keep in view the distinction between faith and assurance. Faith is like the root of our belief, assurance is the flower. You can never have a flower without the root but you can sometimes have the root without the flower. Simple faith in Christ will certainly save a person; yet they may never be free from anxiety and doubts. Faith will bring a soul to heaven but assurance will bring heaven to a soul.

Faith is Peter's drowning cry, *Lord, save me!* (Matt. 14:30). Assurance is that same Peter declaring later to the Council, *He is 'the stone you builders rejected, which has become the capstone.' Salvation is found in no-one else, for there is no other name under heaven given to men by which we must be saved* (Acts 4:11-12). Whoever has faith does well — but whoever has assurance does far better!

69

3. A certain hope is a thing much to be desired

I wish that assurance was more sought after than it is. Too many believers live doubting and die doubting, and go to heaven in a kind of mist.

a) Certainty is to be desired because it gives our souls immediate comfort and peace. Uncertainty in matters of this life, such as family relationships, money or work, can ruin our mental and bodily health. Uncertainty in spiritual matters can ruin the health of our soul.

Assurance will support a believer when loved ones die; it will make it possible to praise God even in difficulty, and to rejoice when suffering for Christ's sake. Assurance made it possible for Peter to sleep soundly the night before he was due to be killed (Acts 12). Assurance removes the ultimate fear; it allows the dying believer to say, *If the earthly tent we live in is destroyed, we have a building from God, an eternal house in heaven* (2 Cor. 5:1).

b) Possession of a certain hope releases a believer's energy for Christian work. Generally speaking, none do so much work for Christ as those who enjoy the fullest confidence of entrance into heaven. A believer lacking assurance will spend much time in searching his or her heart about their spiritual condition. But the believer who, like Paul, has a firm faith and a sure hope, is free from such distractions. Undivided attention to the work will always bring greatest success.

c) Assurance does away with indecisiveness in spiritual matters. Many of those who can only hope they are God's children are continually in doubt about how to behave. Should they do this, or that? Should they go there? Are they never to do this or that? And this is because they are not completely sure whether they are children of God or not! If they knew that the saving work of Jesus was indeed for them, then they would know they are God's child and that would decide their actions.

d) Assurance is to be desired because it makes the holiest Christians. *Everyone who has this hope in him purifies himself, just as he* [Christ] *is pure* (1 John 3:3). A hope that does not purify is a mockery and a delusion.

From what I have said so far it should be clear that the neglect of assurance may be the main reason for all our failures in the Christian life. If that is so with you, then take my advice now. Lay aside your doubts and lean more strongly upon the Lord Jesus Christ. Begin with simply believing Him and assurance will be added.

4. Some probable difficulties in gaining assurance

There are those whose lack of assurance can be explained by one of the following causes. Many believe, but fewer are persuaded; many have faith, but fewer have confidence. Now why is this so?

a) Perhaps there is a defective view of the doctrine of justification. Failure to understand that Christ's work, not our own, is the basis of our acceptance by God will rob us of assurance. Nothing but simple faith is required on our part. Justification is a gift, something entirely apart from ourselves. Simply to believe is to be fully justified. The weakest believer is as completely justified as the strongest believer, and can therefore be assured.

71

b) Perhaps there is laziness about the need to grow in grace. Many appear to think that they can relax and enjoy their new-found faith. They must be reminded that this grace has been given to them as a talent which they must use. Believers need to add to their faith continually (2 Pet. 1:5).

There is an inseparable connection between diligence and assurance (Heb. 6:11; 2 Pet. 1:10). Assurance will never come without diligence in the spiritual life. An important teaching of the Puritans is that 'faith of adherence' (i.e. commitment to Christ — Ed.) comes by hearing, but faith of assurance does not come without doing. 'A lazy Christian will always lack four things; comfort, contentment, confidence and assurance. God has made a separation between joy and idleness, between assurance and laziness; and, therefore, it is impossible for you to bring together what God has put asunder.'[3]

c) Another reason for lack of assurance could be an inconsistent life. Inconsistency of life is utterly destructive to peace of conscience. If you will keep your besetting sins, and cannot make up your minds to give them up, you will never have assurance. *We know that we have come to know him if we obey his commands* (1 John 2:3). Our salvation does not depend upon our works, but the comforting sense of it does depend upon a consistent Christian walk.

I leave these points for your consideration now. They are worth examining carefully.[4]

---

3. Quoted from writing by Thomas Brookes, a Puritan preacher in London, 1654.

4. At this point Ryle gives thirty quotations from Puritan preachers to support what he has said in this chapter. These have been omitted in this abridged version.

Chapter 8. Be like Moses

By faith Moses, when he had grown up, refused to be known as the son of Pharaoh's daughter. He chose to be ill-treated along with the people of God rather than to enjoy the pleasures of sin for a short time. He regarded disgrace for the sake of Christ as of greater value than the treasures of Egypt, because he was looking ahead to his reward (Heb 11:24-26).

To those searching for a pattern of practical holiness, I offer Moses as an example. It seems to me that the way in which faith in God shaped the life of Moses shows us how it could shape our lives. His faith caused him to behave in certain ways very like those ways in which we must behave if we wish to live a consistent Christian life.

1. What Moses gave up

a) He gave up rank and worldly greatness. He refused to be known as the son of Pharaoh's daughter. Because the Egyptian princess had adopted and educated him as her own son, Moses might have been a very important man in the Egyptian court. He could have had rank, power, honour and titles, all those things which so many people eagerly seek! Yet he refused them.

b) He refused pleasures. In the Egyptian court there were pleasures of every kind waiting for him — sensual, social and intellectual pleasures. Egypt was a centre of learning, of art and sciences. Pleasure is something that many spend their lives to achieve. How great a temptation all this must have been for him!

c) He refused riches. The ancient ruins of Egypt give us some indication of the wealth and greatness that once belonged to that country. Moses grew up in Pharaoh's palace. He experienced for himself how comfortable life could be when possessing such riches. What a temptation it must have been to grasp such comfort for himself. Yet, when the time came, he found the strength to turn his back on it all.

2. What Moses chose

a) He chose suffering and affliction. He took the part of his own people — people who were victims of slavery and persecution; for whom there seemed no possibility of deliverance from Egyptian bondage and for whom the likelihood of obtaining a home country for themselves seemed beyond possibility!

We naturally shrink from pain and avoid suffering if we can. But here is a man who, although like ourselves, actually chooses affliction!

b) He chose the company of a despised people. He left the society of the great and the wise, and identified himself with slaves and labourers. He saw a despised people and chose their company rather than that of the noblest people in the land!

c) He chose reproach and scorn. Think of the ridicule Moses would have to endure in turning away from Pharaoh's court to join with the Israelites. There are few things which we find so hard to bear as ridicule and scorn. Yet here is a man who did not shrink from that trial.

And keep in mind that Moses was not a weak or uneducated person, nor was he compelled to make such a choice. What he did, he did freely and voluntarily. Surely this makes his choices as remarkable as his refusals!

3. What made Moses act as he did?

The reason for his unusual behaviour was his faith. He refused all that he refused and chose all that he chose because he believed God. God had revealed to Moses that in the distant future a Saviour was to be born of the Israelite nation, and that the first part of the process leading to that was to happen now, through him. Moses believed what God had said.

a) He believed God would keep His promises, and do exactly as He had said.

b) He believed that nothing was impossible for God to do. Human reason might say that the deliverance of the Israelites was never going to happen. But his faith told Moses that God could make it happen.

c) He believed that God was all-wise. Human reason might tell Moses that he was foolish to throw away all the advantages he had, by leaving Pharaoh's court, but, by faith, Moses understood that if God pointed out a certain way then that way was best.

d) He believed that God was merciful. Human reason might suggest that God could make life easier for the Israelites, but faith told Moses that God was a God of love, and would not give His people one drop of bitterness beyond what was necessary.

e) His faith helped him to understand the true situation the people were in. He knew that greatness in human society is a temporary thing. He knew that there was a reward in heaven for the obedient believer far richer than the riches of Egypt. He knew that trials and suffering could be a means of training believers in the spiritual life. He knew that the Israelites were in fact the people of God's choice.

And was he not right in behaving as he did? The name of Pharaoh's daughter has perished; the city of Pharaoh's palace is not known; the treasures of Egypt are gone — but the name of Moses is still known wherever the Bible is read. He is a great example of the fact that whoever lives by faith is blessed!

4. What practical lessons may we learn from the example of Moses?

a) If you wish to be a true Christian you must choose the way of God and not the way of the world. You must be prepared to accept hard and difficult things, and refuse those easy and comfortable things which are not God's will. The world in our day is like it was in Moses' day — people's hearts are still hardened against God, and God's people are still despised. The important question is, Do you want to be saved? Then remember you must choose whom you will serve. You must come out from the children of this world. You cannot serve both God and the world.

Are you making such sacrifices? Does your religion cost you anything? Are you willing to give up whatever keeps you from God? Is there anything in your way of life which collides with your religion? Or have you smoothed and rounded off everything in your religion to fit conveniently with the way you live? Search and see!

b) The only thing which will enable you to choose God instead of the world is faith. A religion that is to survive must have a living foundation and there is no other but faith. There must be a real belief that God's words are to be trusted however disagreeable they may seem, and that His way is right and all others wrong.

You must learn that promises are better than possessions; that the unseen is better than the seen; that the praise of God is better than the praise of men and women. Then, and only then, will you make a choice like Moses and prefer God to the world. Noah, Abraham, Ruth, Daniel — all these acted as they did because, like Moses, they believed God.

c) The reason why so many are ungodly and worldly people is because they lack faith. They do not really think that what God says is true. There are even many who call themselves Christians who would never think of doing what Moses did.

Such people do not believe in hell, and so do not flee from it. They do not believe in heaven and so do not seek it. They do not believe in the guilt of sin and so do not turn from it. They do not believe they need Christ and so they do not trust Him. They do not feel confidence in God, and so they do nothing for Him. Faith which does not influence our pattern of life is not true faith.

d) The secret of doing great things for God is to have great faith. In your walk with God you will go just as far as you believe and no further. Your peace, patience, courage, zeal and service of God will be no greater than your faith in him.

When you read the lives of great Christians of the past you will find it was their faith which was the inspiration of their holiness. They were so prayerful because prayer is faith talking with God. They were so diligent because diligence is faith at work. They were so courageous because courage is faith doing its duty. They were holy because holiness is faith being made visible.

Do you wish to make it clear that, like Moses, you choose God and not the world? Then go and cry to the Lord Jesus Christ, Lord increase my faith! Faith is the root of a true Christian character. Let your root be right and you will be fruitful. Your spiritual prosperity will always be as great as your faith. Take Moses as your example!

Chapter 9. Lot — A Warning!

He hesitated... (Gen. 19:16)

The Bible, which was written for our instruction, shows us what we should not be like, as well as showing us what we should be like. If we want to be holy, the Bible shows us what to avoid as well as what we should seek. Lot is an example of something to be avoided. His character is summed up in the two words, he hesitated. Even though it was two angels who were urging him to leave the town of Sodom, nevertheless he still hesitated!

1. What sort of a person was Lot?

If I do not make this quite clear, perhaps many will say, 'Ah! Lot was a bad man, a poor unconverted man — no wonder he hesitated.' But Lot was nothing of the kind. Lot was a real child of God, and a justified believer. He was, *a righteous man...* (2 Pet. 2:7). There were defects in his character and he paid dearly because of them. So let us not forget that, like Lot, a believer may have many defects and yet still be a true Christian.

a) We know that Lot lived in a wicked city; he saw and heard lawless deeds and yet was not wicked himself (2 Pet. 2:8). To be a righteous man in Sodom could only be by the grace of God. Without such grace, it would be impossible.

b) Another evidence to his character is that he was *tormented in his righteous soul by the lawless deeds he saw and heard* (2 Pet. 2:8). He was grieved, pained and hurt at the sight of sin. Nothing will account for this but the grace of God.

c) One more evidence of his character is that he was *distressed by the filthy lives of lawless men ... day after day* (2 Pet. 2:7). He did not gradually become so accustomed to the sight of sin that he began to view it with unconcern, as many often do. Again, this can only be explained by the grace of God in Lot.

So do not forget — Lot was a child of God.

2. What do the words *he hesitated* tell us about him?

He understood the appalling morals of the citizens of the city in which he lived; he realised that terrible judgement was about to fall on the city; he knew that God was a God who always kept His word — yet in spite of all this, Lot showed astonishing hesitancy. He believed there was danger, for he had taken the trouble to go to his future sons-in-law and urge them to escape; *Hurry and get out of this place because the LORD is about to destroy the city!* (Gen. 19:14). And yet he hesitated!

He was slow when he should have been quick — backward when he should have been forward — loitering when he should have been hurrying. And yet, remarkable as that may seem, I fear there are many Christians just like Lot! There are many true children of God who, however, know far more than they actually live up to, and understand far more than they sincerely practice. They believe in heaven but seem to care little for it; they believe in hell but little seem to fear it. They hate the devil but often seem to tempt him to come to them. What shall we say of such Christians? They are brothers and sisters of Lot!

a) These are the sort of people who seem to think that real holiness is something beyond their reach. They will agree that holiness is a lovely thing. They like to read about it, and see it in others. But they seem to make up their minds that it is beyond their reach.

b) These are the sort of people who have wrong ideas about love, and rush about trying to please everybody except God. They are afraid of being thought narrow-minded and so try to be agreeable to everybody — forgetting that they ought first to be sure they please God.

c) These are the sort of people who shrink from self-denial and are unwilling to make sacrifices. They seem unable to accept the Lord's command to *take up [the] cross and follow him* (Matt. 16:24).

d) These are the sort of people who hesitate to be strict in their adherence to God's ways, and feel that to mix a little in the ways of the world could do the world good. Yet they do not do good to the world and only get harm to themselves.

A hesitant person is not a happy one!

3. What reasons could account for Lot's hesitancy?

He made a wrong choice earlier in his life. Abraham gave Lot the choice of where to settle with his flocks and his cattle. Lot chose the ground which looked best for his animals, land near to the town of Sodom. He did not ask God if he was doing the right thing by choosing that place. He chose on the basis of worldly wisdom and not on the basis of faith in God.

He mixed with the ungodly when there was no necessity to do so. He *pitched his tents near Sodom* (Gen. 13:12). And the next time we hear of him he is actually living in Sodom (Gen. 14:12). If you make a wrong choice in life — an unscriptural choice — and settle down among ungodly people, the certain result will be damage to your own spirituality. This is the surest way to blunt your feelings towards sin. Beware of needlessly mixing with ungodly people. Beware of Lot's choice!

a) Remember this when you are choosing where to live. Give some thought to what will be helpful to your spirituality. Ask yourself if the gospel message is faithfully taught within easy reach of where you are. Beware of Lot's choice!

b) Remember this when you are choosing your work. It is not enough merely that the wages are good, or that there is a good chance of promotion. Ask yourself whether that work will hinder or help your spirituality. [1]

c) Remember this when you plan to marry. Is your choice of partner a believer? Will your partner draw you nearer to

---

1. At this point, Ryle includes a paragraph seeking to dissuade Christians from being employed on the railways, since railway companies run trains on Sundays. The paragraph has not been included here.

Christ or nearer to the unbelieving world? There needs to be something more than affection and friendship, something more than the possibility of a comfortable home. 'Think', as one old writer has said, 'think and think again, before you commit yourself'. Beware of Lot's choice!

You may think that none of these things really matter if you are a justified believer, one of Christ's people. But let me warn you — your soul will never prosper if you make bad choices at the beginning of your life. True believers will certainly never perish spiritually, but their spiritual life will not thrive if they are always hesitating when they should be decisive.

4. What were the results of Lot's hesitancy?

Some may want to say, 'After all Lot was saved. He was justified — he got to heaven and I want no more than that'. I want to show you one or two things in Lot's history which ought to be thought about, and then perhaps you will see why it is quite wrong to talk as some do.

a) Lot did no good to the people of Sodom. He lived there for many years. No doubt he had many opportunities to speak about the things of God and to try and turn the people from their sin. But he seems to have had no effect at all. Not one righteous person could be found in Sodom, outside the walls of Lot's home.

b) Lot helped none of his relatives towards heaven. We know that he had a wife and two daughters. But it is clear none of them feared God. And when he went to warn his prospective sons-in-law they laughed at him — *his sons-in-law thought he was joking* (Gen. 19:14). Lot shows us what the unbeliever thinks of a hesitant believer!

Lot's wife left the city with him, but she did not go far. She did not have the faith to believe what God had said, or see the need for such a speedy flight. She ignored the clear command not to look back and was turned into a pillar of salt (Gen. 19:17,26). His daughters escaped with him, but ended up causing Lot to commit a wicked sin (Gen. 19:33-36). It is sad to realise that Lot was not the means of keeping even one person from hell.

I am not suggesting that believers who do not linger will be the means of bringing great blessing to the world. Nor do I suggest that believers who do not linger will, as a matter of course, be the means of the conversion of their families. But I do say that it is impossible not to see a connection between Lot's bad choice and his hesitancy, and a connection between his hesitancy and his spiritual uselessness to others.

c) We know very little about Lot after his flight from Sodom. His pleading to go to Zoar and his subsequent departure, and his conduct in the cave, all tell the same story of weakness in grace, and the low state of soul into which he had sunk. We are told of the last days of Abraham, Isaac, Jacob, Joseph and David — but not one word do we find about the sad end of Lot. If we had not been told in the New Testament that he was just and righteous we might well have wondered if he was a true believer at all! We can only think that his example is intended by the Spirit of God to be a warning to all professing Christians. If we are willing to make an outward show of our Christianity let us not hesitate to make an equal spiritual effort in our souls.

I do not want to give you a gloomy view of what it is to be a Christian. My only object is to give you friendly warnings. For we live in days when a hesitant, Lot-like religion is common. It is possible to do many religious things but which require little or no sacrifice; they involve no cross. But to walk closely with God, to be really spiritually minded — to be prayerful, unselfish, quiet, easily pleased, loving, patient and meek — these are still rare things! So I warn you not to attempt what cannot be done, namely, to serve Christ and worldly interests at the same time.

Do you want to know what our times demand? The shaking of nations, the uprooting of old values, the stir and restlessness in people's minds — what do they say? They cry out, 'Christian, do not hesitate!'

Do you want to be found ready to meet Christ when he returns? Your witness bright, your spiritual life active, your Christian courage strong — what does this involve? It involves a refusal to hesitate!

Do you wish to feel a great comfort from your religion? Feel the witness of the Spirit with your spirit, to know certainly that you have believed, not to be a gloomy Christian — how can this be? Do not hesitate about spiritual things!

Do you wish to be useful to your family and to others around you? To draw men and women away from sin, to make your beliefs attractive, to cause your family to say, 'We will go with you' — then do not hesitate in your commitment to Christ!

And let us remember the souls of others as well as our own. If we see Christian brothers or sisters hesitating, let us encourage them. Let us remind one another of the words of God: *Encourage one another daily, as long as it is called Today, so that none of you may be hardened by sin's deceitfulness* (Heb. 3:13).

Chapter 10. A Woman to be Remembered

Remember Lot's wife! (Luke 17:32)

These are words spoken by Jesus Christ when he was talking of His second coming and describing the awful state of many people who would not be ready to receive Him. It is a solemn thing that Jesus had to speak of Lot's wife, when He thought of those lost souls who would not be ready for His return.

What Jesus said is even a more solemn warning when we realise that He was not speaking to the scribes and Pharisees who hated Him, but to His disciples! And notice that He does not say, 'Do not be like Lot's wife', but, 'Remember her'. He speaks as if we were in danger of forgetting the subject; the words are not merely a solemn warning but a plea to stir up lazy memories! I will use three headings to help us give some thought to this matter.

1. The religious privileges which Lot's wife enjoyed

In the days of Abraham, true, saving religion was scarce. There were no Bibles, no ministers of religion, no churches. The knowledge of God was confined to a few families. Most of the inhabitants of the world were living in spiritual darkness, ignorance, superstition and sin. Compared with them Lot's wife had great advantages.

She had a godly man for her husband: she had Abraham — the father of the faithful — for her uncle by marriage. Lot's wife must have been aware of the faith, the knowledge and the prayers of these faithful men. She was probably there when Abraham built his altar between Ai and Bethel (Gen. 12:8). When Lot was taken prisoner by Kedorlaomer, and later rescued by Abraham, she was there (Gen. 14:12). When the angels came to Sodom to warn her husband to flee, she was there (Gen. 19). When the angels took the family by their hands in order to hurry them out of the city, she was there (Gen. 19:16).

But what good effect did all these privileges have on her? None at all! She died graceless, godless, impenitent and unbelieving. In all probability, she conformed outwardly to her husband's religion, but inwardly her heart was wrong in the sight of God — given over to the love of material things. There is much to learn from remembering Lot's wife!

The mere possession of religious privileges will save no one's soul. This may seem a hard truth to those who feel that religious privileges will help them be better Christians. But Lot's wife teaches us that it requires something more than religious privileges to save a soul. Joab was David's captain; Gehazi was Elisha's servant; Demas was Paul's companion; Judas Iscariot was Jesus' disciple — these all died in their sins. We need something more than privileges. We need the grace of the Holy Spirit.

It is right to value religious privileges, but let us not rely on them alone. Let us use them, thankfully, if they are given to us.

If they do us no good, they may do us great harm. The same fire which softens wax hardens clay; the same sun which causes life to flourish in one plant dries up the dead tree. Nothing so hardens our hearts as an unfruitful familiarity with sacred things. We need more than religious privileges!

I give a warning to young people who have had the privilege of godly parents. You cannot enter the kingdom of God on the credit of your parents' religion. You must have the witness of the Spirit in your own hearts. You must have your own repentance, faith and holiness.

2. What was the sin which Lot's wife committed?

We read that, *Lot's wife looked back, and she became a pillar of salt* (Gen. 19:26). Does that seem a small sin? This is the feeling some may have. But there was far more in that look than appears at first.

a) It revealed her true character. Little things often show the state of our minds better than great things. Little symptoms can be the signs of serious disease. One look may demonstrate the state of a person's heart — see Matthew 5:28.

b) It showed her disobedience. The command of the angel was unmistakable, *'Don't look back!'* Lot's wife did not obey. When God speaks plainly by His words in the Scripture our duty is clear.

c) It told of proud unbelief. Lot's wife seemed to doubt that God would do what he had said and destroy Sodom. *Without faith it is impossible to please God* (Heb. 11:6). When anyone thinks they know better than God, their souls are in great danger. If we cannot see the reason for God's dealings with us, our duty is to be silent, and believe.

d) It revealed a secret love of the materialism of this world. She could not leave her home without a backward glance. Her desires were in Sodom, though her body was now outside the city. Her eyes turned towards the place where her treasure was, as the compass needle turns towards the North. *Anyone who chooses to be a friend of the world becomes an enemy of God* (James 4:4). *If anyone loves the world, the love of the Father is not in him* (1 John 2:15).

I believe there never was a time when warnings against unholy worldliness were so much needed by Christians as today (Ryle died in 1900! — Ed.). Lot's wife was no murderer, no adulteress, no thief — but she seemed to be religious, and then she looked back! There are thousands who call themselves Christians yet who fall victims to a love of the materialism of the world. I am sure that it is time for us all to remember the sin of Lot's wife.

a) How many children of religious families begin well and end up irreligious! In childhood, they seemed full of religion. The boy becomes a young man and cares for nothing but amusements and sport. The girl becomes a young woman and cares for nothing but dress and exciting company. They are like Lot's wife.

b)[1] How many young men and women seem to love religion at first but then, little by little, the affairs of this life push out

---

1. This is Ryle's point 'c' and our point 'c' is Ryle's 'b'. We have transposed them for the sake of the logical chronological order, child, youth, adult. His points 'd' and 'e' we have omitted since they were addressed specifically to the Anglican church and therefore not of general interest.

of their minds the things of the life to come. And soon they are behaving like Lot's wife.

c) How many married people do well in religion until their children grow up and leave — and then they fall away. In the early years, they follow Christ diligently. But a spiritual blight comes over them when their children grow up and have to be introduced to adult life. The spirit of the world seems to enter the family. They begin to walk in the steps of Lot's wife.

Beware of a half-hearted religion: beware of following Christ from any secondary motive — to please friends or to appear respectable. Follow Christ for His own sake. Be thorough, be honest, be whole hearted. *No-one who puts his hand to the plough and looks back is fit for service in the kingdom of God* (Luke 9:62).

3. The punishment inflicted on Lot's wife

It is written that *Lot's wife looked back, and she became a pillar of salt* (Gen. 19:26). From living flesh and blood she was turned into a pillar of salt. To die in the best of circumstances and at what could be thought the best of times is still a serious matter. But to die suddenly by the direct intervention of an angry God, to die while in full health and strength, to die in the very act of sin, is a fearful thing indeed!

It was a hopeless end to come to. There was no time even for the briefest of prayers. Such was the end of Lot's wife. Are we to ignore the warning of her end? Think also of such people as Korah, Dathan, Abiram, Hophni and Phineas, Saul, Ahab, Absalom, Belshazzar, Judas Iscariot, Ananias and Sapphira! They were all suddenly destroyed without opportunity for remedy. As they lived rejecting God's word, so they died. They went to meet God with all their sins upon them.[2]

a) Let us understand that the same Bible which teaches that God, in mercy and compassion, sent Christ to die for sinners also teaches that God hates sin and must, from His very nature, punish all who cling to sin and reject the salvation He has provided. The very same chapter which declares God so loved the world also tells us that *whoever rejects the Son will not see life for God's wrath remains on him* (John 3:16,36).

b) Let us understand that there is proof upon proof in the Bible that God will punish the unbelieving, as well as show mercy to the repentant.

c) Let us understand that the Lord Jesus Christ spoke most plainly about the reality and eternity of hell. No lips have used so many words to express the awfulness of hell as the lips of Him of whom it was said, *No-one ever spoke the way this man does* (John 7:46).

d) Let us understand that the comforting ideas which the Bible gives us of heaven have no real meaning if there is no hell. The eternity of hell is as clearly taught in the Bible as the eternity of heaven. Once you allow that hell is not eternal you may as well say that heaven and God are not eternal. The

---

2. At this point, Ryle has several paragraphs pleading for the emphatic preaching of the biblical truth that hell is a reality, concluding with, 'For my part it seems just as easy to argue that we do not exist, as to argue that the Bible does not teach the reality and eternity of hell.' These paragraphs have been omitted here but only because of the full treatment of the subject which follows.

same Greek word is used in the New Testament to express the eternity of both.

If you wish to be a healthy, holy Christian, I ask you to keep the truth of the reality of hell in your thoughts. I ask you to avoid any church ministry which does not plainly teach the reality and eternity of hell. I ask you to consider often what your own end will be. Will it be a hopeless one, like Lot's wife? Let me conclude by asking a few questions to help you think about this subject.

i) Are you careless about the second coming of Christ? The people of Sodom were careless about the warning from God that their city was about to be destroyed.

ii) Are you lukewarm and cold about your Christianity? Are you hesitating between the love of the world and the love of Christ?

iii) Are you secretly loving some sin that you cannot give up? Are you trifling with some 'little' sins?

iv) Are you relying upon having some religious privileges? Are you trusting in your religious knowledge?

v) Are you assuming you will have time to repent later in life? Remember Lot's wife!

May those solemn words of the Lord Jesus Himself affect us deeply. May they quicken us when we are falling back; may they warm us when we are growing cold.

Chapter 11. Christ's Great Power!

One of the criminals who hung there hurled insults at him. 'Aren't you the Christ? Save yourself and us!' But the other criminal rebuked him. 'Don't you fear God,' he said, 'since you are under the same sentence? We are punished justly, for we are getting what our deeds deserve. But this man has done nothing wrong.' Then he said to Jesus, 'Jesus, remember me when you come into your kingdom.' Jesus answered him, 'I tell you the truth, today you will be with me in paradise' (Luke 23:39-43)

I want to try and say something about these verses, which tell the story of the criminal who repented of his sins as he was dying, and was immediately pardoned by the Lord Jesus. There are some important lessons illustrated here.

1. Christ's willingness and power to save sinners

This is the main thing to learn from this story — Jesus Christ is *mighty to save* (Isa. 63:1). The criminal was a wicked man; he was a dying man, he was a helpless man, nailed to a cross. But see what happened when he turned to the Lord in prayer — *Jesus, remember me...*

Our Lord replied immediately! He spoke kindly to the man, cleansed him of his sins, received him graciously, justified him freely and gave him an entrance to paradise. Throughout the whole of Scripture no one ever received so glorious an assurance of salvation as this. And I believe that the Lord Jesus never gave so complete a proof of His power and willingness to save, as He did on this occasion.

In the light of this, do I not have the right to say, Christ will receive any sinner who comes to Him with the prayer of faith? If ever there was a person who seemed too bad to be saved it was this man. Yet mercy was shown to him.

Do I not have the right to say, Salvation is by the grace of God and not through human efforts? This sinner was never baptized; he belonged to no visible church; he never received the Lord's Supper; he never did any works for Christ; he never gave any money for Christian work. But he had faith and so he was saved.

Why then should any man or woman ever despair of salvation, with such a passage as this in the Bible? Whatever state you are in there is still hope. Christ can heal you; Christ can raise you from any depths. Heaven is not shut against you; Christ will still admit you if you will humbly commit your soul into His hands.

If you feel unsure that your sins are forgiven, come to Christ and live. Jesus is full of mercy. I tell you He can do anything needed to save your soul. If you are a believer then do not take credit to yourself — glory in Christ. We do not think highly enough of Him. Do you ever try to do good to others? Then be sure to tell them about Christ. Tell them what He did for this dying criminal. Tell them He can do the same for them.

2. We learn that some are saved at the hour of death, while some are not

There were two thieves being crucified with Christ. What became of the other? Why did he not turn from his sin and pray to the Lord? There is nothing to show that he was worse than his companion; both were wicked men; both were being punished justly. Yet one was taken to paradise; the other was not.

There is warning as well as comfort in this story. The warning tells me that though some may repent and be converted on their deathbeds, some may not. The warning tells me that two people may have exactly the same opportunities for the good of their souls, yet only one may take advantage of those opportunities. The warning tells me that repentance and faith are the gifts of God. If anyone believes that they can repent, believe and come to the Lord at any time they choose, they may find at the end that they are greatly deceived.

Do not presume that God will be merciful. Do not continue in sinful neglect of Him and think you can repent and be saved just when you like. Do not put off for another day anything which concerns the welfare of your soul. Look at the history of people in the Bible ...

Saul and David lived about the same time; rose from similar obscurity in life; they were both called to the same high position in the world; they both reigned for a number of years; both had the ministry of the same prophet, Samuel; yet one was saved and the other was lost.

Do you have any desire to pray? Put it into practice at once! Would you like to serve Christ? Find out how to do so at once! Are you beginning to enjoy Bible truth? Then live up to the truth you learn immediately! You may want to say, 'It's never too late to repent'. But if you keep putting off your repenting you may never repent at all. You may say, 'Why should I be afraid? The penitent thief was saved'. But look again at the story — the other thief was lost!

3. We learn that the Spirit always leads souls to salvation in the same way

It is a mistake to notice merely that this repenting criminal was saved when he was dying. There are other things to notice, such as the evidence of the Spirit's work in this man's heart. The Spirit led him to salvation in the same way that He leads all who are being saved.

a) Notice his faith. He called Jesus by name; he declared his belief in Jesus' kingdom. He believed that Jesus was innocent. Yet he had none of the advantages of being taught these things, as Jesus' disciples had.

And when did he show such faith? It happened when the whole nation had rejected this Christ! It happened when the chief priests and Pharisees had condemned Christ. It happened when Christ's own disciples had fled! Surely this faith was a remarkable faith. Do you want to know if the Spirit is working in your life? Then I ask, Do you have faith such as this, despite the way others reject Christ?

b) Notice his proper sense of sin. He acknowledged his own ungodliness and the justice of his punishment. *We are punished justly, for we are getting what our deeds deserve.* He makes no attempt to justify himself or excuse his wickedness. He speaks like a person humbled by the memory of his past sins. This is what all God's people feel. Do you want to know if you have the Spirit in you? I ask, Do you feel your sinfulness?

c) Notice his brotherly love. He tried to stop his companion from cursing Jesus. There is no surer mark of the Spirit's work than this. He shakes us out of our selfishness and makes us aware of the souls around us. When the Samaritan woman was converted (John 4) she left her water pot and ran to the city saying, *'Come, see a man who told me everything I ever did. Could this be the Christ?'* Do you wish to be certain that you have the Spirit in you? Then I ask, How is your love for other souls?

4. We learn that believers in Christ are with the Lord when they die

This you may gather from the Lord's words, *Today you will be with me in paradise.* Believers, after death, are with Christ. I know their happiness falls short of what it will be when their bodies are raised again when Jesus returns to earth. Yet I know that they do enjoy rest, freedom from labour, pain and sin. They are with Christ.

I cannot describe what kind of a place paradise is, because I cannot understand what it is like when the soul is separated from the body. But when I see that such souls are with Christ, I see enough! If the sheep are with the shepherd — if the members of the body are with the head — if the children of the family are with the one who loves them, all must be well; all must be right.

If you are a believer, if you tremble at the thought of the grave, be encouraged by this passage. You are going to paradise, and Christ will be there.

5. We learn, finally, that the eternal destiny of the believer is very near

Today, our Lord said, *today you will be with me*. Not at some time in the future, but this very day! How near that word brings our everlasting destiny. *There is only a step between me and death*, said David (1 Sam. 20:3). There is only a step, we may say, between ourselves and either paradise — or hell.

We do not realise this as we ought to do. We are apt to think, even as believers, that death begins a long journey. That is very wrong! The moment that believers die they are in paradise. Make no mistake; there is no long interval between death and our eternal condition. The very moment that believers die they are in paradise. If you are a true Christian you are nearer heaven than you think! Today, if the Lord should take you, you would find yourself at once in paradise.

A few words in conclusion. There is encouragement here for the humble hearted sinner. Why should you not do what the repenting thief did? See how he called to the Lord Jesus — and see what an answer he obtained! On the other hand, if you are so proud as to suppose yourself not a sinner, there is a warning here. For the unrepentant criminal died as he lived — a wicked man.

Are you a nominal Christian? Then use the repenting criminal's actions as a test of your own. You will be wise to behave as he did.

If you are mourning over the loss of a believing friend or relative, then take comfort from this Scripture. They cannot be better off than they are now! And if you are an aged servant of Christ, then see how near you are to home! When your king calls for you, in one moment your warfare will be ended and you will be with Him in paradise.

Chapter 12. Knowing Jesus Christ

A furious squall came up, and the waves broke over the boat, so that it was nearly swamped. Jesus was in the stern, sleeping on a cushion. The disciples woke him and said to him, "Teacher, don't you care if we drown?" He got up, rebuked the wind and said to the waves, "Quiet! Be still!" Then the wind died down and it was completely calm. He said to his disciples, "Why are you so afraid? Do you still have no faith?" (Mark 4:37-40)

I wish people — even Christians — would study the four Gospels more than they do. I say this because it is the only way they will ever get to know Jesus. It is good to know about faith and grace, justification and sanctification. But it is even better to know our Lord, for knowing Him leads to holiness. And what better way is there of knowing Him than studying the four accounts of His life as found in the Gospels?

Christ is the spiritual rock on which we must build our lives. Christ is the true vine from whom we must draw spiritual nourishment. Christ is our elder brother from whom we can draw sympathy in times of need. Christ is our advocate to present our prayers before God. Christ is the king in whose kingdom believers spend eternity. So let us see what can be understood of Him, from the story at the beginning of this chapter.

1. We understand that following Christ will not automatically protect us from everyday troubles

The disciples were in great anxiety. Though they were His few chosen disciples — when priests, scribes and Pharisees would not believe in Him — Jesus allowed them to be frightened. Perhaps they had thought that serving Christ would mean that they would escape the common troubles of this life. If Jesus could heal the sick, feed multitudes with a few loaves, raise the dead and cast out devils, surely He would never allow His disciples to suffer. But if they thought so they were mistaken. Serving Christ does not give believers protection from the problems of this life.

It is good to understand this clearly. I have the privilege of being a Christian minister and can speak of the gift of eternal life to any man, woman or child who is willing to have it. But I dare not offer that person worldly prosperity as a part of the Christian message; I dare not speak of long life, freedom from pain, increased wealth. I know many would like to have Christ and good health — Christ and plenty of money — Christ and freedom from all worries. If you are thinking like that you are very wrong. Let me show you why I say that.

How would you ever know if you are a true Christian, if following Christ meant that you never had any troubles? How would you know whether you are following Christ for His sake, or for your own selfishness, if following Him brought health and wealth as a matter of course? How would the great work of sanctification go on in believers if they were never tested by trials? Trouble is the only fire which will burn away the dross that clings to our hearts; it is the pruning knife which cuts away dead wood from our lives and makes us spiritually fruitful.

If you wish to serve Christ, then take Him on His own terms; leave it to Him to decide what is best for you. Be sure that He does everything well.

2. Let us learn that the Lord Jesus Christ is truly human while also truly God

Jesus, we read, was asleep on a cushion. He was a tired man! After preaching in the open-air to huge crowds all day, He was weary. We know how pleasant it is to sleep after being fatigued. And here we read of Him who might have been living in glory with the Father coming to earth to live as a man. He had a body like our own. He was born of a woman. He was often hungry, thirsty and weary. Like us He ate and drank and slept. Like us He sorrowed and wept. He who made the heavens went to and fro as a poor man on earth!

I take comfort from the fact that Jesus is perfect man. Because of this He is not only a great High Priest for me, but also a High Priest who knows how I feel; not only a powerful Saviour but also a sympathetic Saviour; not only the mighty Son of God but also the Son of Man who knows our human sorrows.

I see a marvellous proof of divine love and wisdom in the union of two natures in Christ's person. Marvellous love in our Saviour to be willing to endure weakness and humiliation for our sakes — rebels that we are. Marvellous wisdom, in fitting Himself by His humanity to be the very friend of all friends to us. He can understand all my weaknesses and infirmities and yet also do all that is necessary for my salvation. Had He been only God I might have trusted him, but never could have approached Him without fear. Had He been man only I could have loved Him, but never felt sure He could do everything necessary for my salvation. Deepest sympathy and almighty power are met together in Jesus Christ! Surely every believer has every reason to trust Him.

a) Are you poor and needy? So also was Jesus. He preached from a borrowed boat, rode into Jerusalem on a borrowed ass, and was buried in a borrowed tomb! Foxes have holes, birds have nests, but, He said, He had nowhere to lay His head.

b) Are you alone in the world? So was Jesus. The few that followed Him were fishermen, despised tax collectors and sinners. And even these friends forsook Him in His last hours.

c) Are you misunderstood, misrepresented and persecuted? So was Jesus. He was accused of being friendly with outcast people and base characters. His enemies said He ate too much and drank too much. They said He had a devil and was mad. He was wrongly accused and unjustly condemned to death.

d) Are you sorely tempted? So was Jesus. You can read the account of His temptation in the Gospels of Matthew, Mark and Luke. Do you ever feel that Satan suggests wicked ideas to your mind? So it was for Jesus.

e) Do you ever feel great agony and conflict of mind? Do you ever feel that God has left you? So did Jesus. Who can tell the extent of the suffering He went through in the Garden of Gethsemane and on the cross?

It is impossible to find a Saviour more suited to the wants and needs of our hearts than our Lord Jesus Christ. Do not listen to the suggestion that Mary the mother of Jesus and other saints are more sympathetic than Jesus Christ. Such suggestions spring from ignorance of what the Bible teaches and of the true nature of the Lord Jesus Christ. Whoever finds comfort in the God/Man Jesus Christ needs no comfort from saints and angels or even from the Virgin Mary!

3. Let us understand that there may be a great weakness of faith sometimes, even in true Christians

What more proof do we need of this fact than the behaviour of the disciples during that storm? In fear they woke Jesus, crying out, 'Teacher, don't you care if we drown?' They were impatient — they couldn't wait until He woke; they were unbelieving — how could they have perished with Jesus aboard? They were distrustful — 'don't you care?' they cried!

They ought not to have been afraid. Had they not seen many examples of His love and kindness toward them? But fear often makes us have a bad memory! I am sure many Christians have been in this kind of situation. They think that they are trusting Christ entirely. But when some sudden unexpected trial comes, fear, doubt, and distress break in upon them like a flood.

The truth is that there are no perfect Christians as long as they are in this life. Abraham was the father of the faithful — yet, through fear of the Egyptians, he made his wife say that she was his sister. David had faith enough to face the giant Goliath; he had faith to believe he would one day be God's anointed king of Israel even though Saul pursued him and threatened to kill him. Yet this same David was once so overcome with fear that he thought, *One of these days I shall be destroyed by the hand of Saul* (1 Sam. 27:1).

Does any believer feel such love and confidence in Christ as to be unable to imagine ever being troubled by anything? That is good; I'm glad to hear it! But I ask, Has your faith ever been put to the real test? It is not easy to know your own weaknesses without any testing. The Lord had to leave Hezekiah to show him what his weaknesses were (2 Chron. 32:31). Blessed are those who are 'clothed in humility' in this matter.

I give this word of warning because I want young Christians to understand what they will find in themselves. I want to prevent their dismay when they come up against weakness in themselves. Young believers have to realise that they may well have true faith and grace, and yet sometimes still feel fear and doubt. I want them to look hard at Peter, James and John and know that they were true disciples — and yet not so spiritual that they were never afraid.

Most of all, I want Christians to realise what they may sometimes see in other believers. Do not make hasty judgements. Many a lump of gold is mixed with quartz and dross, yet who thinks gold worth nothing at all on account of that? The disciples in the boat had given up all to follow Jesus; they believed in Him and loved Him. It is possible for a person to forsake all for Christ and yet occasionally to be overtaken with fears and doubts.

4. Let us understand the power of the Lord Jesus Christ

The waves were breaking over the ship where Jesus was. The disciples were terrified. Then Jesus performed a wonderful miracle, such as only the almighty creator could do! You will sometimes feel that you are experiencing a squall! Then it is good to have a clear view of the power of Jesus. Let every believer know that the Saviour is also the almighty One; the Redeemer is also Lord of lords and King of kings. Study the power of Jesus!

a) Study it in His works of creation. *Without him nothing was made that has been made* (John 1:3). All creation, from the sun on high to the meanest worm below was the work of Christ. He commanded — and they began to exist. Was not that great power?

b) Study it in the works of providence. Sun, moon, stars all proceed round in a perfect system. All the seasons follow one another in regular order. The kingdoms of this world rise and increase, decline and pass away at the will of Him in whom *all things hold together* (Col. 1:17).

c) Study the subject in the miracles worked by the Lord Jesus. He could raise the dead with a word; He could give sight to the blind, hearing to the deaf, speech to the dumb — and, supremely, make sinners see and enter the kingdom of God! Look again at the passage which is at the head of this chapter, and learn that Jesus can say to your heart, whatever may be its fear and anxieties, 'Quiet! be still!'

If you long for peace, cry out to Jesus as the disciples did. If you are at peace with God, yet your heart is weighed down by poverty, pain, old age, or the death of a loved one, Jesus can say to your heart, 'Quiet! be still!' Take large views of Christ's power. Doubt anything else if you must, but never doubt Christ's power. One thing is not doubtful, and that is that Christ *is able to save completely* [or *for ever*] *those who come to God through him* (Heb. 7:25).

5. Let us understand how patiently Jesus deals with believers in their weaknesses

There was no anger in the Lord's response to His frightened disciples. *Why are you so afraid? Do you still have no faith?* No sharp rebuke, just two simple questions which throw a beautiful light on the compassion of the Lord. Indeed, the whole of the Lord's conduct towards His disciples deserves close study.

At no time did the disciples seem to fully understand the Lord's teaching. The plainest words and clearest statements of what was going to happen to their Master seemed to have little effect upon their minds. They sometimes quarrelled among themselves as to who was the greatest of them; at another time two of them wished to call down fire from heaven on a village which rejected Jesus. At His arrest, most of them ran away — and Peter denied his Lord three times!

So how did Jesus react to this kind of behaviour? He did not rebuke them as stupid or reject them as cowards. All the time He gently led them on, teaching them little by little just what they could bear. His teaching was always kind, comforting and sensible. There is nothing but kindness, gentleness, patience and love in His dealings with them. I could wish that all the world should know that the Lord Christ is full of pity. He cares for the least of His disciples as well as for the strongest. All believers are given to Him by His Father, and He has undertaken — despite their weaknesses — to bring every one safe to heaven.

My last words in this chapter will be the same as the first. I would like my readers to give much attention to the Gospels, and to the five sections of this chapter. I want everyone to know Christ, and to know Him better, so that they may receive eternal life through Him! Holiness is by knowing Christ better and better.

Chapter 13. Christ's True Church

*On this rock I will build my church, and the gates of Hades[1] will
not overcome it* (Matt. 16:18)

Do you belong to this church, which is built on a rock? Are
you a member of the only true church? These are serious
questions! There are five things in this statement that demand
our attention:

1. A building — My church
2. A Builder — Christ says, 'I will build my church'
3. A foundation — On this rock
4. Perils implied — The gates of Hades
5. Security assured — The gates of Hades will not overcome it

1. The building

This church is not a building; not the Eastern Church or
the Anglican church; not the Baptist church nor church of
Rome. When Jesus speaks of 'My Church' He means all true
believers in the Lord Jesus Christ, all who are converted and

1. **Hades.** In ancient Greek literature, hades was the kingdom of the
    spirits of the dead. The same Greek word is translated in the King
    James Authorised version of the Bible as 'hell'. It is also sometimes
    used to mean 'the grave', or 'death'. In Revelation 1:18 we are told
    that Christ has the keys of it. (From *A Dictionary of Bible Knowledge*,
    published by Grace Publications Trust.)

holy people. He means all who have been born again, who have repented of sin and are being sanctified by the Holy Spirit. All such, of every nation, people, language, tribe and class compose the true and living Church of Christ.

The members of this church do not all worship God in the same way, but they all worship and serve with one spiritual love. They are all led by one Spirit. They are all seeking after the same holiness. Outside this church there can be no salvation.

2. The Builder

This true Church of Christ is tenderly cared for by all three Persons of the Trinity. In the plan of salvation as revealed in the Bible we see that God the Father chooses, God the Son redeems, and God the Holy Spirit sanctifies every member of this church. Nevertheless, it is Christ who is chiefly thought of as the Redeemer of the church.

Believers are *called to belong to Jesus Christ* (Rom. 1:6). *The Son gives life to whom he is pleased to give it* (John 5:21). So Jesus is the Builder of this church.

a) Christ shows great wisdom in building His church. Everything is done at the right time and in the right way. Sometimes the work of building (gathering members into His church) goes on swiftly, sometimes slowly. He makes no mistakes.

b) Christ shows great condescension and mercy as He builds His church. He sometimes chooses the most unlikely persons, and makes them holy people. He often takes the most ungodly people and makes them new people. And He often uses very humble servants as His ministers to take part in this work.

112

c) Christ uses great power in building His church. He carries out the work in spite of opposition and the persecution of His people. In troubled times as well as in good times He continues His work of building unhindered. We should be very thankful that the work of building the church worldwide is in the hands of One so powerful, so merciful and so wise!

3. The foundation

What did the Lord Jesus Christ mean when He spoke of this foundation? Did He mean that the apostle Peter, to whom He was speaking, was this foundation? I think not. If He had meant that Peter was the foundation of the church He would have said, 'Upon you I will build my church'. He went on to say, 'I will give you the keys...' (v. 19), so there is no reason why He should not have said He would build His church on Peter, if that was what He had meant.

No, it was not Peter in person who was meant, but it is Peter's inspired statement about the Lord which is the foundation of the church, *You are the Christ, the Son of the living God* (Matt. 16:16). It is the truth concerning Jesus Christ which is the rock on which the church is built: every member of Christ's true church is joined to the foundation of who Christ is and what He has done.

Without this you will never stand in the day of judgement. To base your salvation upon any other foundation is to build upon sand!

4. Perils implied

Jesus speaks of the gates of Hades. By this He means the power of Satan. The history of the church has always been one of

113

conflict because the evil one hates Christ and all that is to do with Him. That battle never ends in this world. And warfare with the powers of hell is the experience of every member of the true church of Christ. Each one has to fight. The gates of Hades have been continually attacking Christ's people.

a) We must not be surprised at the hostility of the devil. If we belonged to the world[2], the world would love us (John 15:19). As long as the unbelieving world is against Christ it will be against His people. As Martin Luther once said, 'Cain will go on murdering Abel so long as the church is on earth.'

b) We must put on the whole armour of God and so be prepared for the devil (Eph. 6:10-18). That armour has been used by millions of believers like us, and has never been known to fail.

c) We must be patient under the attacks of the devil. The experience of them will help to humble and to sanctify us. It will drive us nearer to the Lord, and wean us away from the world.

d) We must not be depressed by the attacks of the powers of hell. The struggles the true child of God has with the power of wickedness is as much a mark of the grace of God in them, as is the inward peace they may sometimes enjoy. If there is no spiritual conflict in our lives we may well doubt whether we belong to the church on the rock!

---

2. **World.** The word 'world' is used in a number of different senses in the Bible, one of which is, 'A symbol for mankind as it is under the power of sin and Satan and hostile to God'. That is the sense in which the word is used here. (For a full explanation of the ten or so meanings that can be indicated by the word 'world' in Scripture, see *A Dictionary of Bible symbols,* published by Grace Publications Trust.)

5. Security assured

Jesus has given His word that despite all the attacks of the gates of Hades, His true church will continue to stand. It will never be overcome. Great world empires have risen and fallen again; great cities have fallen into ruin — yet the true church of Christ remains. Even churches in earlier years have passed out of existence now, yet others have arisen; the true church lives on in every age. The gates of Hades will never destroy the church entirely, for it has flowing in it the spiritual life of Christ; in that sense it is His body on the earth. Some members of the church may suffer because of the power of unbelievers; they may even be killed. But not all the power of Satan can cast one true believer out of Christ's true church. He to whom believers commit their soul has all power in heaven and in earth. Relatives may oppose you, neighbours may mock what you do, the world may ridicule your faith, but all these will have no strength against the salvation of your soul. All is going on well though our eyes may not see it so, yet.

Strive, then, to live a holy life whatever the consequences. Walk worthy of the true church to which you belong. Or if that is a certainty you do not yet possess, then I say, Come and join the true church. Come and join yourself to the Lord Jesus Christ by faith, without delay. Blessed are they who belong to the church on the rock!

Chapter 14. Christ Requires Churches to be Holy

He who has an ear, let him hear what the Spirit says to the churches (Rev. 2:7)

Whatever the name of your church may be, I invite your special attention to the verse above. If you attend public worship in any Christian church at all these words are for you; they are for all who call themselves Christians.

These words are repeated seven times in the second and third chapters of the book of Revelation. The Lord Jesus sends seven different letters by the apostle John to seven churches in Asia. And each letter ends with these words.

Everything God does is perfectly done — He does nothing without a purpose. Therefore it is certain that no part of the Bible is there by chance. There is purpose and design in every repetition of a verse. There is reason in the sevenfold repetition of these words, and we should therefore pay attention to them. So let me point out the leading truths which are being taught in these seven letters. They are truths for the days we live in — truths which it will be good for us all to know.

1. In all seven letters we find nothing except matters of Christian doctrine, behaviour, warning and promise

Jesus gives a sharp rebuke where He sees false doctrine and ungodly behaviour. Praise is given for faith, patience, good works and perseverance. Repentance and turning back to God is always encouraged.

But I want you to notice that nothing is said about the way churches are governed, or the ceremonies or forms of worship they may use. He does not instruct John to write about baptism, or the Lord's Supper. Now do not misunderstand me, when I say this. I do not say that these things are unimportant. But this I say, all of these things are as nothing compared to faith, repentance and holiness. Those are the first and most weighty matters. I believe that without those spiritual things no one can be saved.

Here is one reason why I so often urge upon people not to be content with the mere outward parts of religion. They are not Christians who are merely so outwardly; there must be a new creation by the Holy Spirit in the heart. True religion is eminently a personal matter between Christ and yourself.

2. Another phrase which occurs in every letter[1] is, *I know your deeds*

It is not for nothing that we read these words seven times! Jesus does not say, 'I know your wishes' — 'I know your decisions' — 'I know what you profess'. He says, 'I know what you do'. It is true that deeds cannot save your soul, but they are important nevertheless. They cannot justify you, or wipe out your sins, but they are a good evidence of the state of your heart. It is of no value if we say that we know God, if our behaviour denies what we say, like those people Paul describes in Titus 1:16. Our behaviour is the evidence of our religion.

---

1. Ryle was using the Authorized (King James) version. The actual words appear in only five of the seven letters in the New International Version but the idea is clearly present in all of them. (Editor.)

a) The Lord Jesus knows the works of unbelievers, and one day will punish them. Such deeds may be forgotten on earth, but they are not forgotten in heaven.

b) The Lord Jesus knows the deeds of His own godly people, and He weighs them. He knows why believers do what they do — how much is done for their own praise, and how much is done for Him!

c) The Lord Jesus knows the deeds of His own people and will one day reward them. He never overlooks anything which is done in His name. The world may not know what you do, or why — but Jesus sees and knows all.

There is a solemn warning in all this. You may deceive others, or even yourself, about what you do and why you do it. But you cannot deceive Christ. But think what encouragement there is in all this, too. You may not feel that you have done very much for Him. All you do seems imperfect, and not as good as you wish it was. But Christ does not forget what you do out of love for Him, however little the world — and even you — may regard it!

3. Another thing repeated in each of the seven letters is a promise to the one *who overcomes*

Seven times the Lord gives the churches great promises. Each one is different, each is full of encouragement, but each one is directed only to 'the one who overcomes'.

Every true Christian meets enemies to the spiritual life of the soul, and must fight them to overcome them. I refer you again to what I said about this in chapter four. The

119

point that I want to make now is that the true believer is not merely a soldier, but is a victorious soldier. Victory is the only satisfactory evidence that any believer has a true saving religion.

a) *Moses ... chose to be ill-treated along with the people of God rather than to enjoy the pleasures of sin for a short time* (Heb. 11:25). This was overcoming the love of ungodly pleasure.

b) Micaiah refused to prophesy smooth things to King Ahab, even though he knew he would be persecuted if he spoke the truth; this was overcoming the love of ease (1 Kings 22).

c) When Daniel refused to give up praying, even though he knew a den of lions was prepared for him, he overcame the fear of death (Dan. 6).

d) Matthew left his tax collector's desk and, at Jesus' call, left all and followed Him. You could say he was overcoming the love of money (Matt. 9:9).

e) Peter and John refused to stop preaching about Christ and His resurrection despite being threatened by the Jewish council. That was how they overcame the fear of unbelieving officials (Acts 4:19-20).

f) Saul the Pharisee gave up all prospect of promotion and high regard among the Jews and went everywhere preaching about the Jesus he once had tried to persecute. This was an overcoming of the love of human praise (Phil. 3:4-9).

The lesson for us is unmistakable. If you wish to make it clear that you are a true believer you too must be prepared for spiritual struggle in God's cause, and overcome!

Let us beware of leaving our first love like Ephesus; of becoming lukewarm like Laodicea; or of tolerating false customs like Pergamum; of tolerating false doctrines like Thyatira or of being halfdead like Sardis. Let us aim for holiness, like Smyrna and Philadelphia. Let us be unmistakably Christian! Let us be truly holy people! Then Jesus will not have urged us to listen to what the Spirit says to the churches in vain.

Chapter 15. Love of Christ is Part of Holiness

Do you truly love me? (John 21:16)

A feeling of love toward someone is one of the common feelings of human nature. Unhappily, people sometimes set their love on unworthy objects. I want to claim a place for the One who is most worthy of our love - Jesus Christ! This is not something which only fanatics do; the very salvation which believers enjoy is only possible because of what Christ has done. How then can believers not love Him? Holiness cannot exist without love for Christ.

There are two points I wish to make on this subject. The first is:

1. The true Christian has a special feeling of love toward Christ

There are many things which Christians believe and do in the course of their Christian lives. But the most notable thing about true believers is their love for their Lord. Bible knowledge, faith, hope, reverence and obedience to God are all things to be seen in a believer's life. But true believers go further than this — they love Christ. A person may lack clear knowledge, may fail in courage, or even fall into sin. But none of these things will lead to your everlasting destruction if you love Christ.

Not believing and not loving are both steps to eternal ruin. *If anyone does not love the Lord — a curse be on him*! wrote Paul (1 Cor. 16:22). Jesus Himself said, to the Jews, *If God were your Father, you would love me* (John 8:42). And after His resurrection, Jesus put this question three times to His disciple Peter, *Do you [truly] love me?* (John 21:15, 16, 17). These are words which probe the reality of our religion. Plain and easy to be understood, these words are most searching words.

If you wish to know the secret of this feeling toward Christ, the apostle John tells us: *We love* [Him] *because he first loved us* (1 John 4:19). We love Him for all that He has done for us. And we love Him for all that He is doing for us at this moment. Believers have been redeemed from the guilt, the power and the consequences of their sins. And every day now they receive from Christ spiritual life and strength, as He prays for them, in heaven.

Does the debtor love the friend who unexpectedly pays his debts in full? Does the drowning person love the one who plunges into the sea and rescues him? Does the person trapped in a burning house love the one who risks his own life to dash into the flames and rescue him? Even a child could answer such questions as these! In just the same way and for similar reasons the true believer loves Christ.

a) This love to Christ is the inseparable companion of saving faith in Christ. If a person has no love for Christ you may be sure they have no true faith in Christ.

b) Love to Christ is the best motive for all work for the Lord. There is a big difference between a nurse caring for a sick child, and the mother caring for her sick child. One acts from a sense of duty — the other from affection and love. One serves because she is paid to do so — the other does what she does because of her heart's love for the child. It is just the same in the matter of service for Christ. The great workers of the church through the ages have all been eminently lovers of Christ.

c) Love to Christ is what we ought specially to teach children. There are many things in Christian truth which will be hard for children to understand. But love to Jesus is something much more within their understanding.

d) Love to Christ is the point at which all Christians, from different branches of the Christian church, can unite whatever their differences in other respects. 'I cannot speak much for Christ', said an old uneducated man, 'but if I cannot speak for him, I could die for him!'

2. How may we recognise a love for Christ?

Since there is no salvation without love for Christ, this is a most important question. But it is not a hard question to answer. How do we know that we love anyone? Let me show you that love for Christ has a similar way of revealing itself as love to our friends and relations.

a) If we love someone we like to think about them. We do not forget them, or need to be reminded of them. They come into our minds many times during a day. In the same way, if we love Christ then, by His Spirit, Christ may dwell in our hearts (Eph. 3:17).

b) If we love someone we like to hear about them. We take notice if their name is mentioned. Those who do not know our loved ones will take little notice when they are mentioned. It is affection which is the secret of a good memory whether among human friends, or between the believer and Christ!

c) If we love someone we like to read about them and to know what they have been doing. Much pleasure comes from a letter from a loved one. It is just so between the Christian and Christ. True believers are delighted to read the Scriptures because there they read about their Saviour.

d) If we love someone we like to please him or her. We find out what they like, and what they dislike, and we try to act accordingly. So Christians make every effort to please Christ; they discover from the Bible what His will is and then seek to do it.

e) If we love someone we also like their friends. When we meet their friends we do not feel we are complete strangers. So, as Christians, all Christ's friends are our friends. We love the same Saviour as they do.

f) If we love someone we will defend them. We do not like to hear anyone talking against them and will immediately defend them. As Christians, we will be hurt to hear anyone speaking against Christ, and want to speak for Him.

g) If we love someone we will like to spend time with them, talking with them, listening to them, or just simply being close to them. However shy and silent we may be toward others we find no difficulty in being with and talking to a close friend. So the true Christian finds no difficulty in talking with Christ.

These are the marks by which true love may be found. They are all plain and simple things, easy to be understood. Use them to examine yourself honestly, and you will know if you have a love for Christ. So let me put to you this question which the Lord asked of Peter, Do you truly love Christ?

It is no answer to tell me that you know all the Christian doctrines. The Bible teaches that there can be no true Christianity without some feeling of love towards Christ. It is no answer to tell me that you disapprove of a religion of feelings. If the religion consists of nothing but feelings then I agree with you; but if you shut out feelings altogether then you know little of real Christianity. If you do not love Christ, it is because you feel no debt towards Him, no obligation to Him. There is only one remedy for this sort of thing. You need a better knowledge of yourself through the teaching of the Holy Spirit. You must find out what your nature really is. You must discover your guilt and emptiness in the sight of God. You must plead with God about your soul. Read how Paul describes human nature in chapters one and two of his letter to the Romans. Study such a passage with prayer for the Holy Spirit's guidance, and you will soon come to understand what I mean about being a debtor to Christ and in need of God's help.

To see your need of Christ is the first step towards loving Him. Not to love Him is to be in imminent danger of eternal ruin. Do not be too proud to accept the advice I offer — take it, and be saved!

There are those who are certain that they love Christ. To those I say, your love is an evidence of God's love, in Christ, to you. You would not love Christ if He had done nothing for you. So never be ashamed to let others see your love for Him. Speak for Him; live for Him; work for Him.

Chapter 16. Separate from Christ

You were separate from Christ (Eph. 2:12)

When Paul wrote his letter to the Ephesians he reminded them that before they became Christians they were, among other things, separate from Christ. But the same words describe any and every person who is not converted to God as a Christian believer. It is bad enough to be without money, or without friends, or without health. But it is far worse to be separate from Christ.

1. When can it be said that a person is separate from Christ?

This condition is not one that I have invented. It was the apostle Paul who first used the expression. No doubt many of the Ephesians were devoted worshippers of the goddess Diana. But Paul thinks nothing of that. Instead he describes the people as without Christ.

a) A person is without Christ when he or she has no knowledge of Him. And millions, no doubt, are in this condition, for they have never once heard of him. There are thousands of people living in England now who have no more idea of who Christ is than those overseas who have never heard of Him

129

(written by Ryle in the 19th century! — Ed.). An unknown Christ is no Saviour.

b) A person is without Christ when they have no faith in Him, even if they have some knowledge about Him. There may be many who have some knowledge about Christ but they make no practical use of that knowledge. They put their confidence in something else. They may hope to reach heaven because of their moral character, or because they sometimes pray, or because they attend church. But they lack an active and trusting faith in Christ; they are separate from Him.

c) A person is separate from Christ when the working of the Holy Spirit cannot be seen in their lives. *If anyone does not have the Spirit of Christ, he does not belong to Christ* (Rom. 8:9). In order to be joined to Christ, knowledge, faith and the graciousness of the Holy Spirit are essential. Those who lack any of these must be separate from Christ.

I want you to think carefully about these three statements which I have just made. So many are ignorant of these things. So many are content to think they have 'been kind to everybody' or that they have 'done their duty'. They talk of 'doing' and never of 'believing'. If you think my statements are too hard and severe I must tell you that they are God's words and not mine. *Whoever does not believe will be condemned* (Mark 16:16). So I must tell you these things, I long to tell everyone of the mercy and loving kindness of God that is available for those who will seek it, for I cannot find anywhere in the Bible that the ignorant, or the unconverted, or the unbelieving are anything other than separate from Christ.

2. What is the actual condition of a person who is separate from Christ?

I can imagine someone saying, 'Well, if I am separate from Christ I am no worse than many others. I hope God will be merciful and that things will be alright at the end.' I want to try to show such people that they are sadly deceived.

a) Separation from Christ means separation from God, for Christ is the only one who can introduce to God ignorant and sinful people who have turned their backs on Him who is their Creator. The holy nature of God is described as 'a consuming fire' to those who are separate from Christ. If we keep ourselves separate from Christ we cannot come close to God. Jesus Himself said, *I am the way and the truth and the life. No-one comes to the Father except through me. If you really knew me, you would know my Father as well* (John 14:6-7).

b) To be without Christ is to be without peace. Everyone has a conscience within them, which must be contented if they are to have peace. In some people the conscience may be half dead, or asleep — in which case it does not cause them much discomfort. But as soon as a conscience has been awakened and is aware of past failings and future judgement, that person finds that something is needed to give inner rest.

There is only one thing which can give peace to a troubled conscience. A clear understanding that Christ's death on the cross was an actual payment for our sins, and that the merit of that death is given to us when we believe, is the grand secret of inner peace! *Since we have been justified through faith, we have peace with God through our Lord Jesus Christ* (Rom. 5:1).

c) To be without Christ is to be without hope. Most people have some sort of hope for themselves in the next life. But very few can give a reason for the hope that they have (1 Pet. 3:15). Such vague hopes will fail to be of use in the moment of greatest need, the moment of death. The only hope worth having is the hope which relies upon Christ and what He has done as our Saviour. There is no such thing as a good hope separate from Christ.

d) It follows from what I have already said that to be separate from Christ is to be without heaven! I do not merely mean that to be without Christ means that you cannot enter heaven, but also that you would be very unhappy if you were there. The joy of heaven is to be with Christ. How can anyone dream of a heaven without Christ? In every description of heaven which the Bible gives us, the presence of Christ is one essential feature. A heaven without Christ would not be the heaven of the Bible.

I could easily add to these things. I could tell you that to be without Christ is to be without life, without strength, without safety, without purpose in life, without a basis for life. There are none so badly off as those without Christ! What the root is to the branches, or the air is to our lungs, as food and water are to our bodies — all this and more Christ is intended to be to us. Nothing is so pitiable as to be without Him!

Chapter 17. Thirst Quenched!

On the last and greatest day of the Feast, Jesus stood and said in a loud voice, "If anyone is thirsty, let him come to me and drink. Whoever believes in me, as the Scripture has said, streams of living water will flow from within him" (John 7:37-38)

In order to appreciate the value of these words, you need to recall the place, the occasion and the time when they were spoken. For it was all of these factors together which drew these words from the Lord.

The place was Jerusalem, the centre of Judaism and the stronghold of the Pharisees and the Sadducees. The occasion was the feast of the Tabernacles, one of the great annual feasts for the Jews, who made every effort to be present in Jerusalem at that time. The time was the last day of the feast, when, according to tradition, water was drawn from the pool of Siloam and poured on the temple altar. [1]

---

1. Bible scholars are divided in their opinion concerning the meaning *of the last and greatest day of the feast.* Some argue that it was the seventh, the climax of the festival; others that it was the eighth, the last festival day of the Jewish year. On each of the seven days, water from Siloam was poured out at the altar of burnt offering, symbolising water from the rock at Meribah (Exodus 17). On the eighth day no water was poured, symbolising the fact that the Messiah had not yet come. Perhaps in that silence Jesus shouted his words of invitation, but this is not certain. (Editor.)

Perhaps Jesus sensed the feeling of anti-climax among the crowds, as the people prepared to return to their homes. He certainly knew that all the ceremonies which had been performed in the temple were just empty rituals. He saw, and pitied the crowds, calling out in a loud voice, *If anyone is thirsty let him come to me and drink!*

Notice the language of Jesus — Come to me. Let me remind you that no other great religious leader has ever used such direct language as this! It is a very positive statement, indicating that Jesus Himself knew that He was the promised Messiah, the Saviour of the world. There are three points in this great saying of the Lord which we should examine:

1. The problem — *If anyone is thirsty*
2. The solution — *Come to me and drink*
3. The promised result — *Whoever believes in me, streams of living water will flow from within*

1. The problem — *If anyone is thirsty*

Everyone hearing Jesus would have known something of the pain of bodily thirst. But how much more painful is thirst of the soul! Physical pain is one thing; but suffering of the mind is more. To have a troubled conscience, to know that we are not ready to meet God, to be aware of our guilt and sinfulness — this is the highest degree of pain. This, no doubt, is the thirst which Jesus is speaking of. It is a thirst for pardon, forgiveness of sins and peace with God. This is the thirst which the Jews felt after Peter preached to them on the day of Pentecost (Acts 2:37). It is the thirst the Philippian jailor felt, when he awoke to his spiritual danger (Acts 16:30).

This is the thirst which many of God's greatest servants have felt, when the light of spiritual understanding dawned upon them. And surely it is not too much to say that all of us ought to know something of this thirst. Lack of feeling in any part of our physical bodies is a sure sign of the presence of death in that part. Nothing proves so conclusively the spiritual death of the minds of men and women than their lack of thirst for peace with God. So Scripture describes unbelieving men and women as spiritually dead — having no feeling towards God. What a terrible thing it is when Jesus has to say to a soul, *You do not realise that you are wretched, pitiful, poor, blind and naked* (Rev. 3:17).

A sense of sin, guilt and poverty of soul is something to thank God for! It is the first sign of the work of the Holy Spirit in a life. It is not when we begin to feel good, but when we begin to feel bad that we are taking the first steps towards heaven; that is the A B C of true Christianity.

2. The solution — *Come to me and drink*

The simplicity of this sentence has to be admired. Here is everyone's answer to the problem of how to have peace with God. This sentence should be kept in mind, along with six other sayings of Jesus: *I am the bread of life; Whoever comes to me I will never drive away; I am the light of the world; I am the gate; I am the way and the truth and the life; Come to me, all you who are weary* (John 6:35; 6:37; 8:12; 10:9; 14:6; Matt. 11:28). Learn by heart these six sayings, together with the one above. Fix all seven in your mind and never let them go! In any time of need you will find them priceless words of comfort!

What is the meaning of all these words? It is that Christ is the source of that spiritual 'living water' which God has provided for thirsty souls. In Christ, as our Redeemer and Substitute crucified for our sins and raised again for our justification, there is an endless supply of every spiritual blessing that we need — pardon, forgiveness, mercy, peace, rest, comfort and hope. So if anyone feels a soul-thirst, let them go to Christ and drink!

Whether a doctor's medicine will help us, or not, depends upon whether we obey the correct instructions for using it. Let me show you the right way to drink from Christ.

a) Those who long for spiritual thirst to be quenched must come to Christ Himself. They must not be content with just going to a Christian meeting, or attending a communion service, or completing some other religious ceremony. If that is all that is done, such people will thirst again. We must deal directly with Christ.

b) Those who are thirsty and want to come to Christ must actually come to Him. It is not enough to wish, to talk, to intend, to resolve or to hope. We must actually commit ourselves to Christ.

c) Those who thirst must remember that simple faith alone is required, in coming to Christ. By all means come in sorrow and repentance for sins committed — but it is not enough to rely merely upon our sorrow for our acceptance with Him. We must also commit ourselves to Him in faith. To drink from Him is to trust in Him, to depend upon Him, to rely upon nothing else but Him for our salvation. Yet, simple as this remedy for spiritual thirst is, how hard it is to persuade people of it! Thank God if you have found it for yourself!

3. The promised result — *streams of living water will flow from within*

Few Christians realise the number and variety of those promises which are to be found in the Bible, for the benefit of those who will use them. Just as promises are the basis of nearly all our human transactions, so promises are the lovely way in which God approaches men and women. Yet there is one big difference between human promises and the promises of God. Human promises may not be kept; the promises of God are always fulfilled.

Many of our human promises are for the benefit of the person to whom they are made. But the promise quoted above seems to refer to many others as well as those to whom the Lord speaks. By speaking of living water flowing from within I believe our Lord means us to understand that we shall not only ourselves have an abundant supply of every spiritual blessing that we need, but also that we shall be a source of spiritual blessing to others around us.

a) Some believers are a source of blessing to others while they live. Their words, their example, their teaching are all means whereby spiritual benefit flows to others. Such were the many great preachers and teachers who were a blessing to thousands while they lived.

b) Some believers are rivers of living water to many when they die! Such are the martyrs of whom we read in the history of the Christian church. The work they did by being faithful unto death was more than they did in their lives!

c) Some believers are a source of blessing to others long after they have died. They still do good by their books and other writings which remain. And again, the good that they do by their writings may be more now than while they were alive.

None of us is converted for our benefit alone; the conversion of a man or a woman often leads on, in God's purposes, to the conversion of others. I doubt if there will be any believers who will not have been to someone or other, a river of living water. And I believe that the resurrection morning will reveal the full meaning of this promise to the astonishment of many who may not be aware that they have been a means of blessing to any!

Chapter 18. Unsearchable Riches

Although I am less than the least of all God's people, this grace was given to me: to preach to the Gentiles the unsearchable riches of Christ (Eph. 3:8)

These are remarkable words, when you consider who it was that wrote them. The writer was none other than the great apostle Paul, a leader of those Jewish Christians who, some twenty centuries ago, turned the world upside down by the message they preached and by the holiness of their lives! Such words from such people demand our attention! There are three important things to notice here:

1. What Paul says about himself — *less than the least of all God's people*
2. What Paul says of his authority to preach — *this grace was given to me*
3. What Paul preaches about — *the unsearchable riches of Christ*

1. What Paul says about himself

He was the founder of many churches, the writer of fourteen inspired epistles[1], a worker of miracles, a man who suffered

---

1.   **Inspiration**. By 'the inspiration of Scripture' we mean that the whole of Scripture has its source in God; it is 'breathed out' by God (2 Tim. 3:16). This does not commit us to believing that God merely dictated the Scriptures. Rather, we understand that He created the

beatings, stonings, shipwreck and many other dangers for Christ's sake — but what does Paul say of himself? *I am less than the least of God's people*. What a poor thing the least person is — yet Paul thinks of himself as even lower!

This humility is beyond the comprehension of many who call themselves Christians, who are nevertheless without true Christian experience. They cannot understand the conflicts, the fears, the hopes, the sorrows of the true Christian. Just as the blind cannot appreciate works of art and the deaf cannot enjoy music so the unconverted person — whether claiming to be Christian or not — cannot understand this sort of spiritual humility.

But Paul meant what he wrote. In other places he writes even more remarkably, *I am the worst of sinners* (see 1 Tim. 1:15). *What a wretched man I am! Who will rescue me from this body of death?* (Rom. 7:24). By the teaching of the Holy Spirit Paul saw things wrong in himself which the unconverted person never sees in themselves.

And this spiritual humility is a feeling which every true believer is aware of. The more knowledge of God Christians have in their hearts the deeper is their sense of sin. The more they understand the holiness of God so the more they are conscious of their own unholiness, and the less likely they are to think themselves perfect. This is a humility to be sought!

What have we to be proud of in ourselves? Of all the creatures born into this world, none are so dependent as are human beings. Physically who needs so much care and attention as we? Mentally how ignorant the greater portion of the human race is, and what misery we make for ourselves

writers with their different personalities and circumstances in order to use them in this task of writing the Scriptures as He wanted it written. (From *A Dictionary of Theological Terms*, published by Grace Publications Trust.)

by our foolishness! Surely we ought to be the most humble of all the creatures on the earth. The more humility we have the more Christlike we shall be, for it is written of Him that He *made himself nothing ... he humbled himself* (Phil. 2:6-8).

Heaven, I suppose, will teach us fully how humble we ought to be. Once we understand more clearly how we have been saved, and led through life, and brought to enjoy such heavenly glory we shall completely realise the wonder of what God has so graciously done for us, His believing people, and then the sort of humility which Paul shows us will seem so right!

2. What Paul says of his authority to preach

It is evident that Paul regarded the main work of the apostles to be the passing on of the good news of the Christian message by preaching. He makes this clear in others of his writings: *I was appointed a herald* (1 Tim. 2:7); *of this gospel I was appointed a herald* (2 Tim. 1:11). In another place he says *Christ did not send me to baptise, but to preach the gospel* (1 Cor. 1:17).

I believe Paul understood that the principal work of a Christian minister is to be a preacher. Nowhere does he suggest that a Christian minister is ever to be a priest; indeed, nowhere in the New Testament is a Christian minister spoken of as a sacrificing priest, as the Roman Catholic church requires its ministers to be for the offering of the sacrifice of the Mass. [2]

---

2. **The Mass**. The word refers to the Lord's Supper as celebrated by the Roman Catholic Church, in which the priest is considered to be participating in the sacrifice of the body and blood of Christ, by believing that the bread and the wine become them, thus making the timeless and eternal sacrifice of Christ visible in the present here and now. (From the *Evangelical Dictionary of Theology*, published by Marshall Pickering.)

Paul's last instruction to Timothy, whom he had left in charge of a church, was *'Preach the Word!'* (2 Tim. 4:2).

a) Let us be clear in our minds that the work of preaching is required of a minister by the Scripture. This is clear from those passages of the New Testament which we have already noticed. No honest reader of the letters to Timothy and Titus can come to any other conclusion than that preaching is a biblical practice.

b) Let us be clear in our minds that preachers are useful gifts wisely given to us from God. God is a God of order, who works by using human means; we have no right to expect Him to work by a constant flow of miracles. There is no better plan for the continual preaching of God's truth and for maintaining God's requirements in the churches than that He should raise up those who are faithful preachers.

c) Let us be clear in our minds that to be a preacher is a great privilege and also a serious responsibility. It is an honour for a person to be the ambassador for a king; how much greater the honour to be an ambassador for the King of kings! It is also a serious responsibility rightly to represent the one for whom they are ambassadors. To be unfaithful, to fail to deliver less, or to say more, than the true message these are faults that bring disgrace to an ambassador. *I have caused you to be despised and humiliated before all the people, because you have not followed my ways* was the sad word God had to speak to some leaders in Israel (Mal. 2:9).

How we need to pray earnestly for those who are preachers, that they should be faithful to God's word. And how we should often plead with God to raise up more and more faithful preachers!

3. What Paul preaches about

That Paul should preach about Christ is no surprise for it was Christ in all His glory that met Him on the road to Damascus (Acts 9:3-4). After that Paul never wasted his time talking about anything else! But what did he mean when he spoke about *the unsearchable riches of Christ*?

a) There are unsearchable riches in Christ as a person for He was both God and Man. This is a great mystery, no doubt. But the thoughtful Christian can never be ashamed to believe that Christ is both human and divine. If He had been only human then He could not save us from our sin. If He had been only divine then He could not have experienced our temptations and weaknesses. As God He is mighty to save; as Man He is exactly suited to be our representative. Though an inexhaustible truth, it is also a precious truth that Christ is both God and Man.

b) What Christ has done for us by His death, resurrection and ascension is unsearchable. He completed the work His Father gave Him to do (John 17:4): the work of atonement, reconciliation, redemption, substitution as 'the just for the unjust' and the complete satisfaction of God's righteous demands of us. Each of these words is so rich in meaning!

c) There are unsearchable riches in the various ministries which Christ fulfils for His people. He is their mediator, their advocate, their high priest, their shepherd, their physician, their captain, their king, their master, their head, their forerunner, their elder brother! To those believers struggling to live the life of faith all these ministries are unsearchable riches!

d) There are unsearchable riches in the names and titles that belong to Christ. I cannot here list them all, but the careful reader of Scripture will find there titles such as the Lamb of God, the bread of life, the door, the way and the truth and the life, the vine, the rock, the cornerstone. To the unbeliever these are all meaningless words; but to the believer unsearchable riches are here!

e) What Christ intends for His people is something of unsearchable richness. There is richness of power to pardon, forgive, cleanse; a richness of patience, sympathy, strength and glory to come. The believer will know that there are no riches to equal these things in any other person than in Christ.

And all these riches are unsearchable — they are like a mine where new treasures are constantly being discovered. The best of believers knows so little of this Saviour! But to know something of this Christ is life eternal. Those who have the Son of God have life; those who do not have the Son of God do not have life (1 John 5:12). When we come to glory, we shall be astonished at how imperfectly we had known these unsearchable riches of Christ, and at how little we had really loved Him. So let us seek to know Him better now for this is the road to holiness.

Chapter 19. What our Times Require of us as Christians

... men ... who understood the times (1 Chron. 12:32)

There was a time in the Old Testament history of Israel when the tribes were divided in their loyalty between king Saul's family (after he had been killed in battle) and David, whom God had anointed as the next king. But one of the tribes — that of Issachar came forward boldly in support of David. And they are given this special word of praise — men who understood the times.

I suggest that, like them, it is important for us to know and understand the times in which we live. To be content to sit ignorantly in one's own private circumstances and to ignore what is going on in the Christian church and in the world, is to be a poor kind of Christian. Next to our Bibles and our own hearts, our Lord would have us study our own times.

In the New Testament, the Lord Jesus Christ rebuked the Jewish people of His day for not recognising the times (Matt. 16:3; Luke 19:44). All ages have their dangers for Christians and each age needs Christians who recognise those dangers. *If the trumpet does not sound a clear call, who will get ready for the battle?* (1 Cor. 14:8).

1. The times in which we live require us to maintain the entire truth of Christianity and the authority of the Bible as God's Word

The words which a famous bishop wrote in 1736 are still remarkably true today:

It is come to be taken for granted by many persons, that Christianity is not even a subject for enquiry; but that it is now, at length, discovered to be fictitious. Accordingly they treat it as if, in the present age, this was an agreed point among all people of discernment, and nothing remained but to set it up as a subject of mirth and ridicule, as it were by way of reprisals for its having so long interrupted the pleasures of the world. (From the Introduction to Bishop Butler's *Analogy of Religion.*)

In newspapers, magazines, books, lectures and sometimes even sermons, writers and speakers are still making war against the foundations of Christianity. Philosophers, and scientists constantly tell us that no educated person can believe a supernatural religion, or the entire Bible, or the possibility of miracles. Such truths as the Trinity, the deity of Christ, the personality of the Holy Spirit, the existence of the devil and the reality of heaven and hell are, by many, thought of as rubbish. And all this is done so cleverly that weak Christians can be influenced by it.

Such unbelief should not surprise us. Ever since the time of Adam and Eve the devil has worked unceasingly, tempting people not to believe in God (Luke 18:8; 2 Tim. 3:13; 2 Pet. 3:3). But as I tell you not to be surprised at so much unbelief, I urge you not to be shaken in mind by it.

Christianity will survive all the attacks by clever unbelievers. When such sceptics have done all that they can, we must not forget the three great facts that cannot be explained away.

a) The first is the fact of Jesus Christ Himself. If Christianity is not true, and not from God, how do these sceptics explain Jesus Christ? How do they explain His appearance in human history? How do they explain that, without force or bribery, He has left such a marked impression upon the world? How is it there has been no one like Him from the beginning of human history? Nothing can explain Him, except what the Bible says of Him.

b) The second fact is the Bible itself. How is it that this book is what it is? How is it that a book apparently written by a few Jews in a remote part of the earth, at greatly different periods of history and without authors knowing each other, still exists because of its own merit — a book so deep, so simple, so wise, so free from defects? This can only be explained if the book is supernatural and from God.

c) The third fact is the effect which Christianity has had upon the world. If Christianity is merely a human invention, and not God's word, how is it that it has made such a difference to the state of human kind? How else can sceptics explain the moral difference in the condition of humanity before and after its coming? How do we explain the differences between the countries where Christianity has been present, and those where it has not? Only the fact that Christianity brings the knowledge of God's truth and holiness to us, can explain its impact upon the world.

2. The times in which we live require from us firm and clear ideas of Christian doctrines

I cannot keep silent about my fears that our religion can be as much damaged by carelessness within the church about matters of doctrine, as from without by sceptics and unbelievers. Many who say they are Christians seem very uncertain about what is right and wrong doctrine. They are easily influenced by clever preachers or by new and attractive ideas. The only certain thing about such people is that they dislike being certain about Bible truths!

These people are living in a kind of spiritual mist, in which they see nothing clearly. The danger is that they will drift to their graves without any comfort or hope from their religion. And the explanation of this condition is not hard to find. The human heart is naturally blind to the beauties of spiritual religion, and is not interested in searching after religious truth. We like to be thought of as very tolerant, and easy-going. And the result is that we tend to favour being less than distinct in our beliefs.

I do implore all who read these words to beware of this undecided state of mind in religion. The victories of Christianity have always been won by clear doctrinal theology. We must teach people clearly of Christ's death and what it means, we must teach the ruinous nature of sin, of justification by faith, of regeneration by the Spirit, of the need to repent and give themselves to Christ. This is the sort of distinctive teaching which God has honoured with success through the centuries.

3. The times in which we live require from us a higher standard of personal holiness and an increased attention to practical religion in daily life[1]

Since the days of the Reformation[2] there has never been so much failure to follow a high standard of Christian living as now. The way to a higher standard of holiness is not difficult to find. Some may even smile at my simplicity. We need to examine more closely the ten commandments of God. We need to examine much more closely the Sermon on the Mount spoken by Jesus. We need to read more carefully the second half of many of Paul's epistles.

A common complaint in these days is of a lack of power in modern Christianity. I believe the reason for this is the lower standard of life which is so prevalent among many Christian believers. The Holy Spirit sees that and is grieved; the world around us sees it and despises us. We need more

---

1. Ryle's point 3 has been omitted here, so that our point 3 is his point 4, our 4 is his 5. In his point 3, Ryle presents a very strong attack on the Roman Catholic Church, making it the great enemy of true religion in his day. That section has been omitted here, despite the fact that we affirm that some of the teachings of that Church are not drawn from Scripture; what is more, a number of their teachings have been drawn from past traditions which are now regarded as possessing the authority of Scripture. Today, it would be our view that the great enemies of true religion are many more; they include, in addition to the teachings of Roman Catholicism, Pluralism, Postmodernism, New Age thinking, the Occult, Apathy toward religion, and Biblical illiteracy, none of which were so prominent in the good bishop's day as they now are. (Editor.)

2. **The Reformation**. The Reformation of the sixteenth century was an historical movement when believers broke away from the Roman Catholic Church and made Scripture the only standard for their beliefs and practices. (From *A Dictionary of Theological Terms*, published by Grace Publications Trust.)

men and women who are walking with God as did the saints of Bible days! Where is our self-denial, our separation from worldly things, and refusal to seek extravagant luxury? Let us set ourselves much higher standards of holy living.

4. The times in which we live require from us a steady perseverance in getting good for our souls

Let us never forget that whatever we may do in the way of public religious activity, it must be accompanied by private religious practice. It is not that I want to see a decrease in public acts of religion, but I do want to see an increase in private acts of religion — religious activity between each believer and God. The times require of us all more attention to our private devotions.

a) Let us pray more earnestly in private. When believers fail to be Christlike in public it is because they had long before neglected their private devotions.

b) Let us give more attention to our Bible reading. Ignorance of Scripture truth will lead to many mistakes in our thinking and make us an easy prey for the devil.

c) Let us cultivate the habit of private meditation. We need time to sit quietly and take stock of our spiritual condition, to have communion with God and to think about Bible truths. Spiritual prosperity depends immensely upon our private devotions. *Go into your room, close the door and pray* is a saying of Jesus much neglected these days (Matt. 6:6).

Can I leave you with some questions now? For example, do you see the particular dangers of the time in which you live? And in the light of them, are you making sure that you do those things which will be for the good of your soul? Beware of indecision about doctrinal truth in the name of liberality and tolerance. *Be all the more eager to make your calling and election sure* is the advice Peter gave to believers who lived in a time when there were many false teachers troubling the churches (2 Pet. 1:10).

And lastly, in view of the spiritual dangers of the time in which you are living, are you doing all that you can for the spiritual good of the souls of others? There is much to be done, so use every opportunity that you can for evangelising others. Remember that God often works with the humblest of His servants. Be determined not to go to heaven alone!

Chapter 20. Christ is All ...

Christ is all, and is in all (Col. 3:11)

The words of this statement are few, short and soon spoken. But they are full of meaning for the true believer. They are the essence and substance of Christianity. If we understand them in our hearts, then we may be confident that our faith is leading us in the right direction. That is why I purposely close this volume with a chapter on this remarkable statement. Whoever seeks after holiness will make no progress unless Christ is given the right place in their thinking.

1. Let us understand that Christ is all, in all God's thoughts concerning the human race

a) There was a time when this world did not exist. The mountains, the seas, the stars, none of them had come into being. There were no living creatures, no human beings. Where was Christ then? Even then Christ was with God, and was God, and was equal with God (John 1:1; Phil. 2:6). Jesus spoke of a glory He had, before the world was: *Father, glorify me ... with the glory I had with you before the world began* (John 17: 5). And even then, Christ was the Saviour — Peter wrote that we *were redeemed ... with the precious blood of Christ, a lamb without blemish or defect. He was chosen before the creation of the world* (1 Pet. 1:18–20).

b) There was a time when the world was created in its present form. Sun, moon, stars, sea, land and all creatures were created — and last of all Adam, the first man, was formed of the dust of the ground. Where was Christ then? Read what the Bible says: *Through him all things were made; without him nothing was made that has been made* (John 1:3). And later Paul was to write, *For by him all things were created: things in heaven and on earth* (Col. 1:16). In Hebrews chapter one and verse ten we can read, *In the beginning, O Lord, you laid the foundations of the earth, and the heavens are the work of your hands.* So are you surprised that our Lord continually taught lessons taken from the natural world? When He spoke of the sheep, the fish, the birds, the corn, the fig tree and the vine, He was speaking about things He Himself had made!

c) There was a day when sin entered the world through the disobedience of Adam and Eve. They lost the holy nature which they possessed at their creation. They lost the friendship and favour of God and became corrupt and helpless sinners. Their sin became the barrier between themselves and their heavenly Father. If He had dealt with them then as they deserved there would have been nothing for mankind descended from them to hope for, except death and everlasting hell. Where was Christ then?

It was on that very day that Christ was revealed as the only hope of salvation for sinners. God said to the serpent, *I will put enmity between you and the woman, and between your offspring and hers; he will crush your head, and you will strike his heel* (Gen. 3:15). In other words, a Saviour born of a woman would overcome the devil. Never has any other name been known to have done this than the name of Jesus Christ.

d) There was a time when the nations of the earth had become ignorant of God. The Egyptians, Assyrians, Persians, Greeks, and Romans had all become immersed in superstitions and idolatry. Poets, historians, and philosophers had all shown that with all their intellectual powers they could not discover the true God. *In the wisdom of God the world through its wisdom did not know him* (1 Cor. 1:21). Except for a few Jews, the whole world was spiritually dead in ignorance and sin. What did Christ do then?

He left the eternal glory He had with God the Father and came to this ungodly world to provide a way of salvation for such sinners. He took our human nature for Himself and was born as a man. As a man, He did the will of His Father perfectly, as we should have, but could not do, because of our sin. On the cross, He suffered the wrath of God that we should rightfully have suffered. And so He brought into the world a righteousness of His own, by which now He can redeem sinners. *He was delivered over to death for our sins and was raised to life for our justification* (Rom. 4:25). He ascended to be again with His Father, and from there He now gives salvation to all who will come to Him in simple and believing trust.

e) There is a time coming when sin will be banished from this world. There will be a new heaven and a new earth. *The earth will be full of the knowledge of the LORD as the waters cover the sea* (Isa. 11:9). And where will Christ be then? What shall He do? He will be King! He will come again with great power and glory and the world will be His kingdom. To Him every knee will bow, and every tongue will confess that He is Lord. His

155

kingdom will be an everlasting kingdom, never to pass away or be destroyed. The whole earth will be His! See what the Bible has to say about this wonderful time: Ps. 2:8; Dan. 7:14; Matt. 24:30; Phil. 2:10,11; Rev. 11:15.

f) There is a day coming when every human being will be judged. The sea will give up the dead that are in it; death and hell will give up the dead that are in them; all will be judged according to the way they had lived. And where will Christ be then? Christ Himself will be the judge! *We must all appear before the judgment seat of Christ, that each one may receive what is due to him for the things done while in the body, whether good or bad* (2 Cor. 5:10).

Surely we shall do well to think about these things. Whoever thinks little of Christ thinks very differently from God the Father! In all God's thought about the affairs of this world and its people, Christ is given the place of honour. To think little of him is to despise one of whom God thinks most highly. It is no wonder that we read, *He who does not honour the Son does not honour the Father, who sent him* (John 5:23).

2. Let us understand that Christ is all in every book which makes up the Bible

Christ is to be found in every book of both the Testaments — indistinctly in the early books, more clearly in the middle and completely in the last of the books — but really and plainly everywhere. Christ's sacrifice on the cross, and His kingdom are the things we must keep in mind when reading any part of Scripture. It is He who is the key for understanding many of the difficult passages of the Bible. Let me show you what I mean:

a) It was the sacrifice and crucifixion of Christ which was being illustrated in the animal sacrifices of the Old Testament. They showed how the sacrifice of a substitute for the sinner could bear away sin by the shedding of blood; *without the shedding of blood there is no forgiveness* (Heb. 9:22). Remember also the significant words of Jesus: *This is my blood of the [new] covenant which is poured out for many for the forgiveness of sins* (Matt. 26:28).

b) It was the sacrifice of Christ which Abel illustrated when he offered a better sacrifice than his brother Cain (Gen. 4). In offering an animal from his flock as a substitute for himself, Abel showed that he understood that without the shedding of blood there is no forgiveness.

c) It was Christ of whom Enoch prophesied during the great wickedness of men and women before the flood of Noah's day, when he said, *See the Lord is coming with thousands upon thousands of his holy ones to judge everyone* (Jude 1:14-15).

d) It was Christ of whom Abraham was thinking when he believed God's promise that through one of his descendants all nations would be blessed. As Jesus said to the Jews, *Your father Abraham rejoiced at the thought of seeing my day; he saw it and was glad* (John 8:56).

e) It was Christ of whom Jacob spoke to his sons, as he lay dying, when he foretold that, *The sceptre will not depart from Judah, nor the ruler's staff from between his feet, until he comes to whom it belongs and the obedience of the nations is his* (Gen. 49:10).

f) All the ceremonies of the law which God gave to Israel were designed to teach them of the work of Christ, the Messiah who was to come. The morning and evening sacrifices, the continual shedding of blood, the tabernacle furniture, the high priest, the Passover, the day of atonement, the scapegoat — all these were patterns of Christ and His work.

g) All the miracles which daily took place in the presence of Israel in the desert as they left Egypt were illustrations of the work of Christ. The guiding pillar of cloud and fire, the manna from heaven, the water from the rock, the brazen serpent on which people looked to escape death from the bites of the poisonous serpents — these and others were all meant to teach the nature of the ministry of Christ (1 Cor. 10:4).

h) It was Christ of whom all the judges were examples, as they were raised up to be saviours of the people in distress.

i) It was Christ of whom king David was a pattern. Chosen to be king while few gave him honour and respect, despised and persecuted by many of his own people, yet in the end a great and victorious king — these are all things which remind us of Christ.

j) It was Christ of whom all the prophets, from Isaiah to Malachi, spoke. Sometimes it was His sufferings, sometimes it was of His glory that they spoke. Sometimes they were inspired to speak of His first humble coming, sometimes of the glory of His second coming. Sometimes they saw both comings and spoke of them as if they were one, but it was always Christ who was in their minds.

k) The New Testament is full of Christ. The Gospels tell of His living among His people; the Acts are of Christ being preached by early believers, the Epistles give careful explanation of Christ's teachings, the Revelation describes the end to which Christ will bring all things.

Whenever you study the Bible, I urge you to remember that Christ is all and in all!

3. Let us understand that Christ is all in the religious experience of every true Christian

In saying this I do not mean to suggest that other biblical truths, such as the doctrine of the Trinity, or the doctrine of God the Father's election of His people, or the doctrine of the Holy Spirit making those people holy, are unimportant. I am quite sure that every believer on reaching heaven will praise and magnify the blessed Trinity of Persons in the Godhead, Father, Son and Spirit.

Nevertheless, I see clear proof in the Scriptures that it is the intention of God that Christ should be particularly concerned in the matter of saving souls. His birth and His death are the basis of all salvation. Christ is the way and the door by which every believer must come to God. Paul wrote to some believers *God was pleased to have all his fulness dwell in him* (Christ) (Col. 1:19). What the sun is to our sky, so Christ is to Christianity.

a) Christ is all in the justification of a sinner in God's sight. How can any of us be acceptable in God's sight? Not because of anything we have done! We are all guilty of breaking God's laws. So how can we approach God? We can come in no other way than in the name of Jesus, pleading that He died for the ungodly and that we trust in Him. His is the only name, the only merit, by which anyone can gain heaven.

Let us never forget that Christ must be all to any who would desire to be justified in God's sight. We must be content to go to heaven as spiritual beggars, depending only upon the grace of God and His gift of salvation to all whose faith is in Christ alone.

b) Christ is all in the believer's sanctification. Do not misunderstand me when I say that. I do not mean to underrate the work of the Holy Spirit who indwells believers. But what I am saying is that no one is ever holy until they have first come to Christ and been united to Him by faith. Jesus Himself said, *Apart from me you can do nothing* (John 15:5). No one can grow in holiness unless they are at one with Christ.

c) Christ is all in the comfort of believers in this life. Believers have sorrows just like other people. They have bodies which are just as weak as others. They have sensitive natures - perhaps more so than many. They have bereavements to bear, worldly thinking to oppose, a blameless life to live. They are sometimes persecuted, and like everyone else they have to die. But such Christians have one great encouragement; they have the *encouragement from being united with Christ* (Phil. 2:1). Christ is the friend that sticks closer than a brother; He alone can adequately comfort His people. How a believer endures the troubles of life may appear wonderful, but the reason is that Christ gives wonderful consolation.

d) Christ is all in the Christian's hopes for the future. Nearly everybody has personal hopes for the future. But most of those hopes have no solid basis. The unbeliever has no certainty about hopes for the future. The Christian's hopes for the future are based upon the fact that Jesus Christ is coming again — coming to gather together all His family to be for ever with Him. So believers can wait patiently for the future. They can bear hard things without grumbling because they are waiting with the certain knowledge of their Lord's return.

Believers can be moderate in all things now because they know that their treasure is in heaven, their good things are yet to come! This world is not our rest; but a hotel. A hotel is not a home. Christ is coming; heaven is coming — and that is enough. *Find rest, O my soul, in God alone; my hope comes from him* (Ps. 62:5).

4. Let us understand that Christ will be all in heaven

It is not easy to speak on this point, for I cannot say much about a world unseen and unknown, such as heaven! But this I know that all men and women who reach heaven will find that even there also, Christ is all.

Like the altar in the Tabernacle and Temples of the Old Testament, the wounds of the once crucified Christ will be the grand object of praise in heaven. In the midst of the throne of God there will be One like the *Lamb, looking as if it had been slain* (Rev. 5:6). The song of all the inhabitants of heaven will be, *Worthy is the Lamb, who was slain, to receive power*

161

and wealth and wisdom and strength and honour and glory and praise! (Rev. 5:12).

The presence of Christ will be all, in heaven. We shall see His face, hear His voice and speak with Him as friend to friend. His presence will satisfy all our wants. The service of the Lord Jesus Christ will be the perpetual occupation of the inhabitants of heaven. At last believers will be able to work for Him without distraction, and serve Him without weariness.

What a sweet and glorious place heaven will be to those who have loved the Lord Jesus while here on earth. But, sadly, many who talk of going to heaven when they die have no real acquaintance with Christ. They give Him no honour here, so what will they do in heaven? They have no communion with Him here, so what will they do in heaven? They do not enjoy spiritual things here, so how will they ever find joy in heaven?

I hope I have begun to show you what deep meaning there is in the phrase Christ is all. There is more I could have said. For example, Christ should be all in the life and worship of every Christian church. Splendid ceremonies, beautiful buildings, armies of professional clergy, all these are nothing if the Lord Jesus is not honoured supremely. The church where Christ is not all is only a dead carcass.

I could make the point that Christ ought to be all in the teaching of every Christian ministry. Christian preachers and teachers are to be ambassadors to carry the message to an unbelieving world about the King's Son, and if they teach people to think more about anything else then they are not fit to be Christian preachers and teachers. God will never honour a ministry which does not teach that Christ is all.

I might also show how the Bible seems to exhaust language in describing all the various ministries of the Lord Jesus. High priest, mediator, redeemer, Saviour, forerunner, surety,

captain, the Amen, the almighty, mighty God, counsellor
— all these and many more are names given to Christ in
Scripture. The ways in which the fullness of Christ is described
seem almost endless!

Is Christ all, to you, my reader? If not, then learn from what
I have said here the utter uselessness of a Christless religion.
Is Christ all to you? If not, then learn from what I have said
here the utter uselessness of seeking to add anything to what
Christ has done in the matter of the salvation of sinners. You
must never think that salvation is by Christ, and something
you have done. That is to change God's plan of salvation in
which Christ is all.

Is Christ all to you? If not, then apply directly to Christ
now! It is not looking at the lifeboat which saves the
shipwrecked sailor, but actually getting into it. It is not
looking at bread which saves the hungry person, but actually
eating it. So it is not knowing about Christ, or even believing
that He is a Saviour which will save you, unless there is an
actual transaction between yourself and Him, a deliberate
committing of yourself to Him. You must be able to say
'Christ is my Saviour, because I have come to Him in trust
and faith, and taken Him for my own'.

'Much of religion', said Martin Luther, 'turns on being able
to use possessive pronouns. Take from me the word "my" and
you take from me my God!'. Let us live on Christ. Let us live
with Christ. Let us live to Christ. So doing we shall attain
great peace, and prove that *without holiness no-one will see the
Lord* (Heb. 12:14).

Epilogue

Bishop Ryle's teaching is biblical and for this reason is as helpful today as it was when his book was first published. There is no need to change anything in this book. However, changes in the moral standards of our society and in the sort of problems faced today by the churches make it necessary to think through the application of biblical principles to these additional situations unknown in his day.

We have no doubt that Ryle would heartily approve of any attempt to speak directly to our present situation. Thus, for example, we think the good Bishop would be happy with our responses to the following questions:

1. Is it helpful to holiness, and in line with the teaching of Scripture, to make — as some do — the requirements of love conflict with the demands of God's law?

We do not think it is helpful to suggest this. It is true that *love is the fulfilment of the law* (Rom. 13:10) but that is not the same as saying that love is above the law. Today, one often hears it argued that sex outside of marriage, and adultery, are acceptable as long as there is true love present. We are told that homosexual practices are acceptable so long as there is loving consent between the participants. It is argued that abortion on demand is acceptable if love and compassion are the motives. We are told that love and compassion can justify the legalisation of euthanasia.

We are asked to consider that genetic engineering of body parts and even 'cloning' of human beings could be acceptable, in the light of suggested benefits to mankind — without any reference to possible abuse, or the will of God, the Creator.

In all these situations, it is becoming common to argue that the motivation of love can justify disregarding or actually disobeying the clear teachings of the Scripture. With the consequence that the result (which ought not to surprise us), sometimes immediately, but always ultimately, is — hurt, distrust and disintegration of the God-given foundations of a stable society.

When Paul says *love is the fulfilment of the law*, he does not mean that we are to abandon the laws of God, but that our love for others will be shown by our keeping His laws and following His commands in all our relationships.

2. Is it a sign of spiritual health and maturity to look — as some do — for direct leading from the Holy Spirit, rather than to use our minds to apply biblical principles when seeking the will of God on difficult issues?

We doubt whether this is a sign of spiritual health. We gladly agree that the Bible tells of many examples of direct guidance from God. It is clear that God could use the same methods nowadays. But it is also clear that with the coming of the completed Scripture, after Pentecost, such happenings were not always the case. The apostles did not seek God's direct intervention in their lives, nor did they teach the early churches that this was necessary. Direct intervention came only when God deemed it necessary. The teaching of Scripture for us is that God shows us His will by instructing us through biblical guidelines and giving us understanding of them by the Holy Spirit who indwells believers (Ps. 32:8; Eph. 5:17).

In Romans 12:1-2 Paul gives us the basic principles by which we should discover God's will. First, there is to be a total dedication to Him. Second, there is to be a total rejection of ideas based upon the unbelieving world's unbiblical standards. Third, there is to be the use of the thinking of spiritually renewed minds — that is, minds saturated with Scripture and prayerfully submissive to God. There is no spiritual profit in the by-passing of our minds.

When we are compelled to grapple with such issues as gambling, lotteries, television viewing, our place of employment, marriage and its breakdowns etc., we are to think through these issues in the light of Bible teaching. To search the Scripture — and to search our own hearts — which this use of our minds will involve, can be a means of our growing in grace and holiness.

As life becomes increasingly complex and pressurised, and society becomes increasingly lawless and corrupt, the way of holiness will become increasingly difficult to sustain. Let the principles taught in this book and these additional comments be firmly fixed in our minds, for they will serve us well in the hour of temptation or of decision.

Clifford Pond

GRACE
ESSENTIALS

THE EXPERIENCE
THAT COUNTS

JONATHAN EDWARDS

THE EXPERIENCE THAT COUNTS

Jonathan Edwards

What does it mean to be a Christian? Is Christianity a matter of the intellect alone? What about desires, feelings and experiences? What is conversion? These questions are not new, Jonathan Edwards, the great American theologian tackled these, and many others, against the background of the First Great Awakening.

These questions, and the answers Edwards gives to them are profoundly relevant to us today.

Find 'a guide for the perplexed' – a voice of clear biblical and spiritual sanity to lead us safely through the maze of contemporary confusion in this crucial area.

The spiritual value of Jonathan Edwards' Religious Affections can hardly be exaggerated. But the difficulty of the subject matter, combined with Edwards' tedious writing style and eighteenth century vocabulary, makes digesting it quite challenging for the modern reader. I am delighted that Christian Focus is releasing this modern edition of Edwards' classic work. Read this book. Let it read you. You will be challenged, convicted, and changed. I commend it highly.

Timothy K. Beougher,
Billy Graham Professor of Evangelism and Church Growth,
The Southern Baptist Theological Seminary, Louisville, Kentucky.

Edwards shows such humanity and realism as he tackles the issue of our emotional life. But he does so with great biblical clarity and charity, walking the tightrope between constraint and freedom. This is one of those books that every Christian should read more than once!

Mark Meynell,
European Director of Langham Preaching, London.

ISBN 978-1-78191-719-0

GRACE
ESSENTIALS

BIBLICAL CHRISTIANITY
THE INSTITUTES OF THE
CHRISTIAN RELIGION

JOHN CALVIN

Biblical Christianity
The institutes of the Christian Religion

John Calvin

Through exploring in turn the Father, the Son, and the Holy Spirit, Calvin's *Institutes* sought to achieve a 'knowledge of ourselves' in light of 'knowledge of God'. This work, foundational to theological thought for five centuries, is presented here in a faithfully edited version — perfect for enriching Bible Studies or devotionals.

John Calvin's Institutes of the Christian Religion stands like a majestic castle in the history of the Protestant Reformed tradition. Many Christians, intimidated by its size and scope, stand outside its gates, honoring it from a distance and wondering what lies inside. Here is an opportunity to wonder no more! Th is new edition of the reformer's magnum opus opens up the warmth and light of the Institutes to any reader. Scaled down in size and updated in language, this version serves up central aspects of Calvin's greatest work with such clarity that you will wonder why you waited so long to enter in. Read, feast and rejoice!

R. Carlton Wynne
Assistant Professor of Systematic Theology and Apologetics
Westminster Theological Seminary
Philadelphia, Pennsylvania

ISBN 978-1781-91965-1

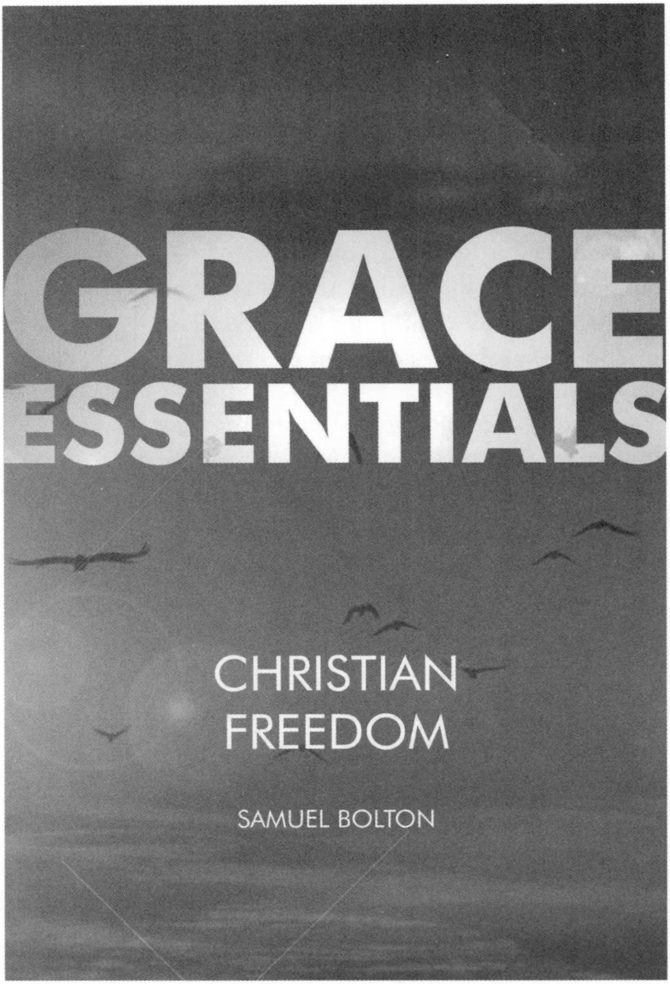
GRACE
ESSENTIALS
CHRISTIAN
FREEDOM
SAMUEL BOLTON

CHRISTIAN FREEDOM

Samuel Bolton

Christian Freedom provides an accessible entry into Samuel Bolton's original work, *The True Bounds of Christian Freedom*, first published in 1645. This book is not simply an academic discussion; Samuel Bolton constantly reminds his readers of the gospel, and the great transformation that has happened to a person who has trusted in Jesus Christ. Bolton shows us clearly that real Christian obedience comes from a changed heart, and is motivated by love for God. He deals with the practical question of what happens when Christians fall into sin, and encourages us to rely on what Christ has done for us, rather than on our performance.

This modernization of an important work by the seventeenth-century Puritan Samuel Bolton addresses certain key questions of the Christian life and answers them in the solidly Biblical fashion we have come to expect of a Puritan author. Especially helpful is the way that he outlines the nature of true Christian freedom: what we have been delivered from and how God expects us to use our freedom. And what is most needed at the present day: he shows us that liberty and obedience are not polar opposites but two sides of the Christian coin.

Michael A. G. Haykin
Professor of Church History and Biblical Spirituality
The Southern Baptist Theological Seminary
Louisville, Kentucky

ISBN 978-1781-91721-3

Grace Publications Trust

Grace Publications Trust is a not-for-profit organisation that exists to glorify God by making the truth of God's Word (as declared in the Baptist Confessions of 1689 and 1966) clear and understandable, so that:

- Christians will be helped to preach Christ
- Christians will know Christ better and delight in Him more
- Christians will be equipped to live for Christ
- Seekers will come to know Christ

From its beginning in the late 1970s the Trust has published simplified and modernised versions of important Christian books written earlier, for example by some of the Reformers and Puritans. These books have helped introduce the riches of the past to a new generation and have proved particularly useful in parts of Asia and Africa where English is widely spoken as a second language. These books are now appearing in editions co-published with Christian Focus as *Grace Essentials*.

More details of the Trust's work can be found on the web site at *www.gracepublications.co.uk*.

Christian Focus Publications

Our mission statement –

STAYING FAITHFUL

In dependence upon God we seek to impact the world through literature faithful to His infallible Word, the Bible. Our aim is to ensure that the Lord Jesus Christ is presented as the only hope to obtain forgiveness of sin, live a useful life and look forward to heaven with Him.

Our Books are published in four imprints:

CHRISTIAN FOCUS

popular works including biographies, commentaries, basic doctrine and Christian living.

CHRISTIAN HERITAGE

books representing some of the best material from the rich heritage of the church.

MENTOR

books written at a level suitable for Bible College and seminary students, pastors, and other serious readers. The imprint includes commentaries, doctrinal studies, examination of current issues and church history.

CF4•K

children's books for quality Bible teaching and for all age groups: Sunday school curriculum, puzzle and activity books; personal and family devotional titles, biographies and inspirational stories – because you are never too young to know Jesus!

Christian Focus Publications Ltd,
Geanies House, Fearn, Ross-shire,
IV20 1TW, Scotland, United Kingdom.
www.christianfocus.com